Backyard Pollinators

Clouded and orange sulphurs, red clover, and helianthus
Carla Schmakel

Ruby-throated hummingbird and sakura cherry blossoms
Dorie Petrochko

Backyard Pollinators

Cordelia Norris, Tiffany Miller Russell
& Trudy Smoke Robbins

Backyard Pollinators

Text ©2021 by Cordelia Norris
Tiffany Miller Russell & Trudy Smoke Robbins
Joseph Cadotte, ed.

Interior illustrations ©2021 by their respective artists
Front cover illustration ©2021 by Amanda Surveski
Cover and interior design ©2021 by Cordelia Norris
Back cover illustration ©2021 by Sami Hernandez

All rights reserved. No part of this book may be reproduced or transmitted in any form or by any means, electronic or mechanical, including photocopying, recording or by any information storage and retrieval system, without prior permission in writing from the publisher.

Luna Creative
Wilmington, North Carolina 28409
lunacreates.com

OTHER WORKS IN THE
COLORING WONDER SERIES

Hatchlings: A Coloring Book Anthology
with Suzanne Matheson

All Along the Atlantic: From Open Ocean to Cypress Swamp
with Cathy Meyer

Costa's hummingbird and agave
Charon Henning

TABLE OF CONTENTS

Anatomy of a flower 1
Taina Litwak

Magnified pollen 3
Christina Spence Morgan

Turtle grass and crustaceans 5
Cordelia Norris

White-banded crab spider and white snakeroot 7
Tiffany Miller Russell

Minute pirate bugs and leafy spurge 9
Chelsea Housand

Snow pool mosquito and blunt-leaved orchid 11
Taina Litwak

Fungus gnats and jack-in-the-pulpit 13
Jennifer Deutscher

Bee fly and Virginia spring beauty 15
Carol Schwartz

Blue bottle flies and eastern skunk cabbage 17
Carol Creech

Bird hover fly and stream orchid 19
Deborah Shaw

Bristle flies and feverfew 21
Taina Litwak

Western tiger swallowtails and Canada thistle 23
Vicky Earle

Silver-spotted skippers, yellow coneflower, and white wild indigo ... 25
Carla Schmakel

Common buckeyes and chrysanthemum 27
C Olivia Carlisle

Painted lady, common eastern bumblebee, and sunflower 29
Amelia Svec

To Start

Unexpected Pollinators

Flies

Butterflies

Butterflies

Monarch butterflies and milkweed 31
Amanda Surveski

Marine blue butterfly and fairy duster 33
Karin Lakshmi von May

Moths

Yucca moths and Joshua tree 35
Taina Litwak

Clouded crimson moths and scarlet beeblossom 37
Maria Klos

Garden tiger moths and common burdock 39
Trudy Smoke

Wasp moths, thrips, and lantana 41
Samantha Gallagher

Sphinx moths and red valerian 43
Chelsea Housand

White-lined sphinx moth and Rocky Mountain columbine 45
Carrie Carlson

Tobacco hawk moth and coyote tobacco 47
Megan Wilson

Snowberry clearwing moth, painted lady, and field thistle 49
Amanda Surveski

Bees

Dunning's miner bees and pussy willow 51
Samantha Gallagher

Bicolored sweat bees and large-flowered tickseed 53
Susan Fox

Short leafcutter bees and New England aster 55
Erin Avery

European honey bees and American white water lily 57
Cass Graybeal Brown

Royal lady bees and Christmas vine 59
Aissa Domingo

Rusty patched bumblebee and goldenrod 61
Alison Burke

White-shouldered bumblebee and subalpine larkspur 63
Carrie Carlson

Bees

Half-black bumblebee and pink lady's slipper orchid 65
Mattias Lanas

Yellow-banded bumblebees and obedient plant 67
Sami Hernandez

Cactus bees and fishhook barrel cactus 69
Karin Lakshmi von May

Wasps

Virginia flower fly, American hoverflies, wild carrot wasps, and Queen Anne's lace 71
Courtney Werner

Pollen wasp and Scott Valley phacelia 73
Aissa Domingo

Great golden digger wasps and coralberry 75
Carla Schmakel

Great black wasp, common eastern bumblebee, and wild bergamont 77
Lauren Rosenfelt

Beetles

Goldenrod soldier beetles and tall boneset 79
Lauren Rosenfelt

Red checkered beetle, notch-tipped flower longhorn beetle, Venus flytrap, and yellow pitcherplant 81
Claire Alderks Miller

Sap beetles and star magnolia 83
Bea Martin

Cycad weevil, pleasing fungus beetle, atala butterfly, and coontie ... 85
Tiffany Miller Russell

Red megacerus and hedge bindweed 87
Bea Martin

Red milkweed beetles and milkweed 89
Gabriela Sincich

Birds

Baltimore oriole and coral tree 91
Clara Hunt

'Apapane, 'amahiki, o'hia lehua tree, and koa tree 93
Susan Fox

White-winged dove and saguaro cactus 95
Carol Schwartz

Birds

Allen's hummingbirds and red bush monkey-flower 97
Sara Lynn Cramb

Calliope hummingbird and firecracker penstemon 99
Charon Henning

Ruby-throated hummingbirds and trumpet vine 101
Hannah Loeffelholz

Lucifer hummingbird and ocotillo 103
Charon Henning

Blue-throated mountain-gem, red yucca, and velvet mesquite 105
Karin Lakshmi von May

Other Invertebrates

Gold dust day geckos and Chinese hibiscus 107
Sami Hernandez

Green anoles and saw palmetto 109
Megan Wilson

Mexican long-tongued bats and century agave 111
Erin Packard

Lesser long-nosed bat and cardon cactus 113
Sami Hernandez

Common opossum and canudeiro 115
Madi Henline

Contributors 117

Bumblebee
Hannah Loeffelholz

To Alan and Leslie for all their support and love
—Trudy Smoke Robbins

To Steve, thank you for your help and your enduring confidence
—Tiffany Miller Russell

To Joseph and our most charming little guy, Jacab
—Cordelia Norris

Island marble butterfly and mustard plant
Laurie O'Keefe

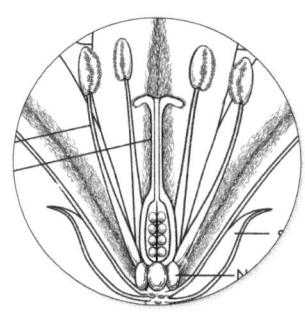

Anatomy of a flower

Taina Litwak, illustrator

Pollination is the life-sustaining relationship between flowering plants, the angiosperms, and the pollinators in our backyards, farms, fields, and everywhere that plants are found. While they come in many shapes, sizes, and colors, all flowers have some parts in common that enable pollination. Flowers have evolved amazing shapes and strategies to enable pollination and begin their cycle of reproduction.

In early spring, buds develop, swell, and grow into flowers. These buds are the protective outer covering known as sepals, which may be green like leaves or similarly colored to the future petals. Petals are the brightly colored parts of the flowers that attract us as well as pollinators. Many flowers are monoecious, with both male and female reproductive structures in the same flower but others are dioecious and contain only male parts or only female parts.

The stamen is the male part of the flower. It is made of filaments or thin stalks topped with pollen-filled anthers. The pistil is the female part of the flower that contains the stigma, the † part at the top that collects deposited pollen grains from the style or pollination tube. The pollen grains travel down to the ovary which produces ovules, the female reproductive cells that become seeds once fertilized.

Flowers have ingenious ways of attracting pollinators, whether they are insects, birds, or mammals. Some flowers have scented nectaries, which produce the sugary nectar that draws in pollinators. Some have special landing platforms for pollinators to rest on as they eat the nectar and pollen, some have colorful markings that serve as nectar guides to help pollinators find nectar and brush against the pollen at the same time, and some flowers change colors to signal that they contain nectar.

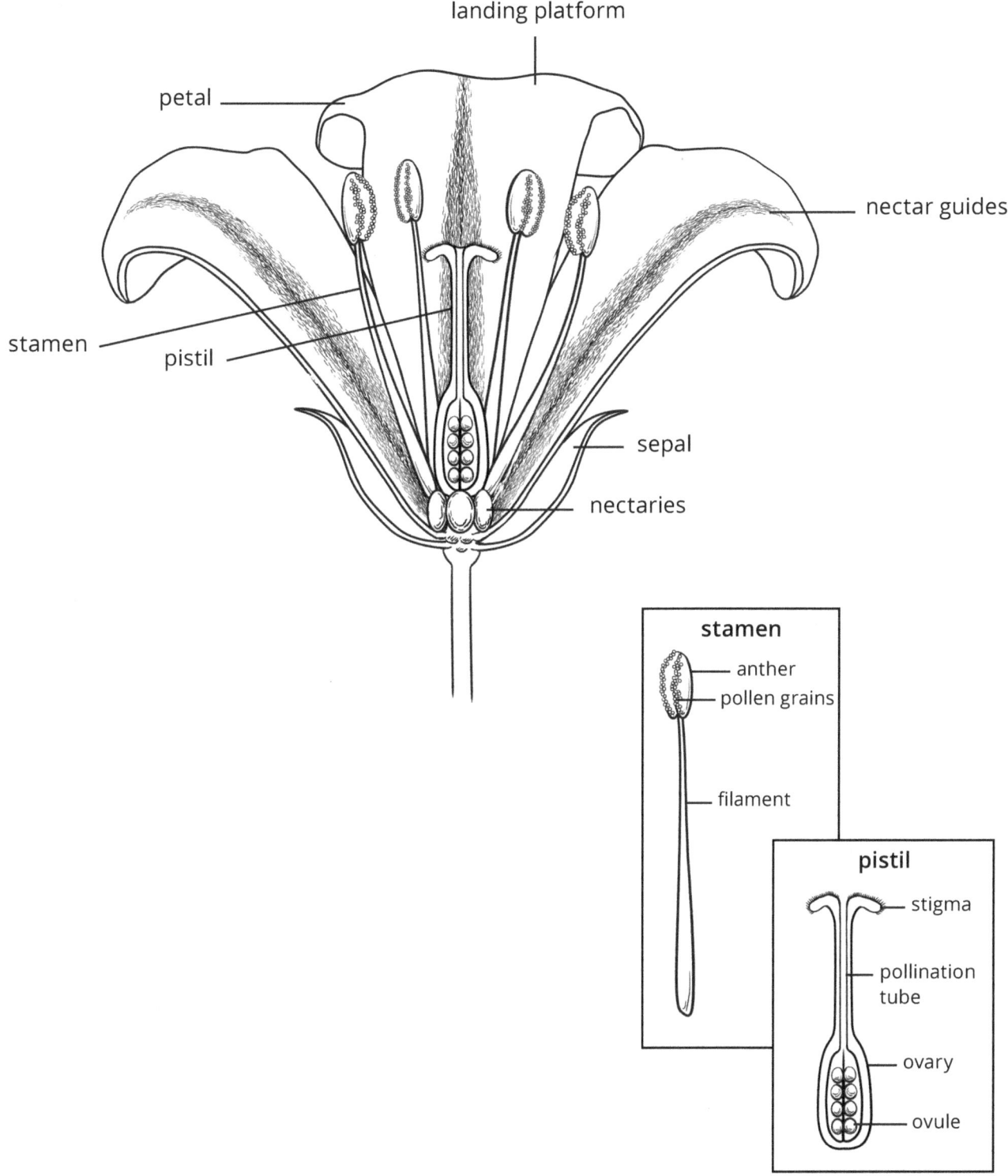

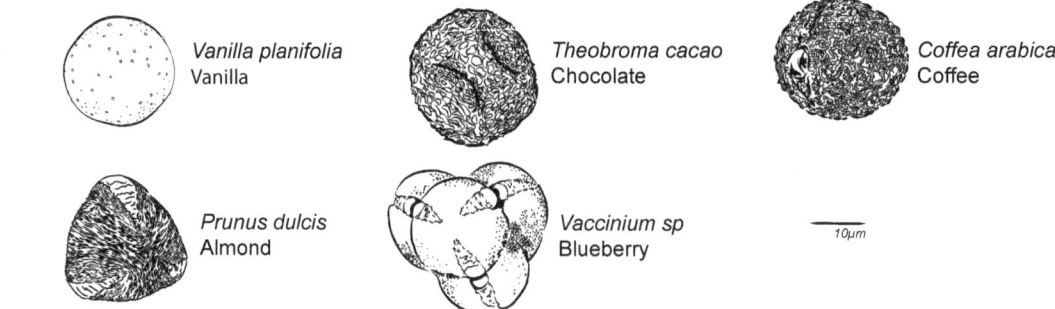

Under the microscope

Christina Spence Morgan, illustrator

Plants produce pollen as part of the male aspect of reproduction. Each pollen grain consists of one to a few cells that contain the male microgametophytes. To the naked eye, pollen looks like yellow or white dust. The compound microscope and the Scanning Electron Microscope (SEM) have given us new insights into the surface anatomy of pollen grains.

Magnification at many thousands of times reveals the unique characteristics and beauty of each plant pollen species. The shapes, sizes, and ornamentation of each tiny pollen grain differ, and each is a work of art specific to a particular plant. Paleontologists use fossil pollen to identify the plant communities present millions of years ago. They can also identify what flowers pollinators have visited by scraping the pollen off of pollinators and looking at it under a microscope. The uniqueness of pollen shape and size prevents many plants from cross-pollinating unrelated species.

Pollinators come in many forms, from insects like bees and butterflies, beetles and flies, to birds, reptiles, and mammals. They typically visit flowers to feed on nectar or pollen, becoming dusted with pollen grains in the process. While investigating the next flower, the pollinator drops some grains on the flower's stigma, pollinating it. Pollen is usually sweet-smelling and mild, although some plants produce foul-smelling pollen that's irresistible to certain insects.

Many pollinators also ingest pollen, or in the case of some bees and other insects, use it to make "loafs" of pollen and nectar to feed their young. Pollen is an important source of protein, along with fats, starches, vitamins, and minerals. For some pollinators, it's their main source of protein.

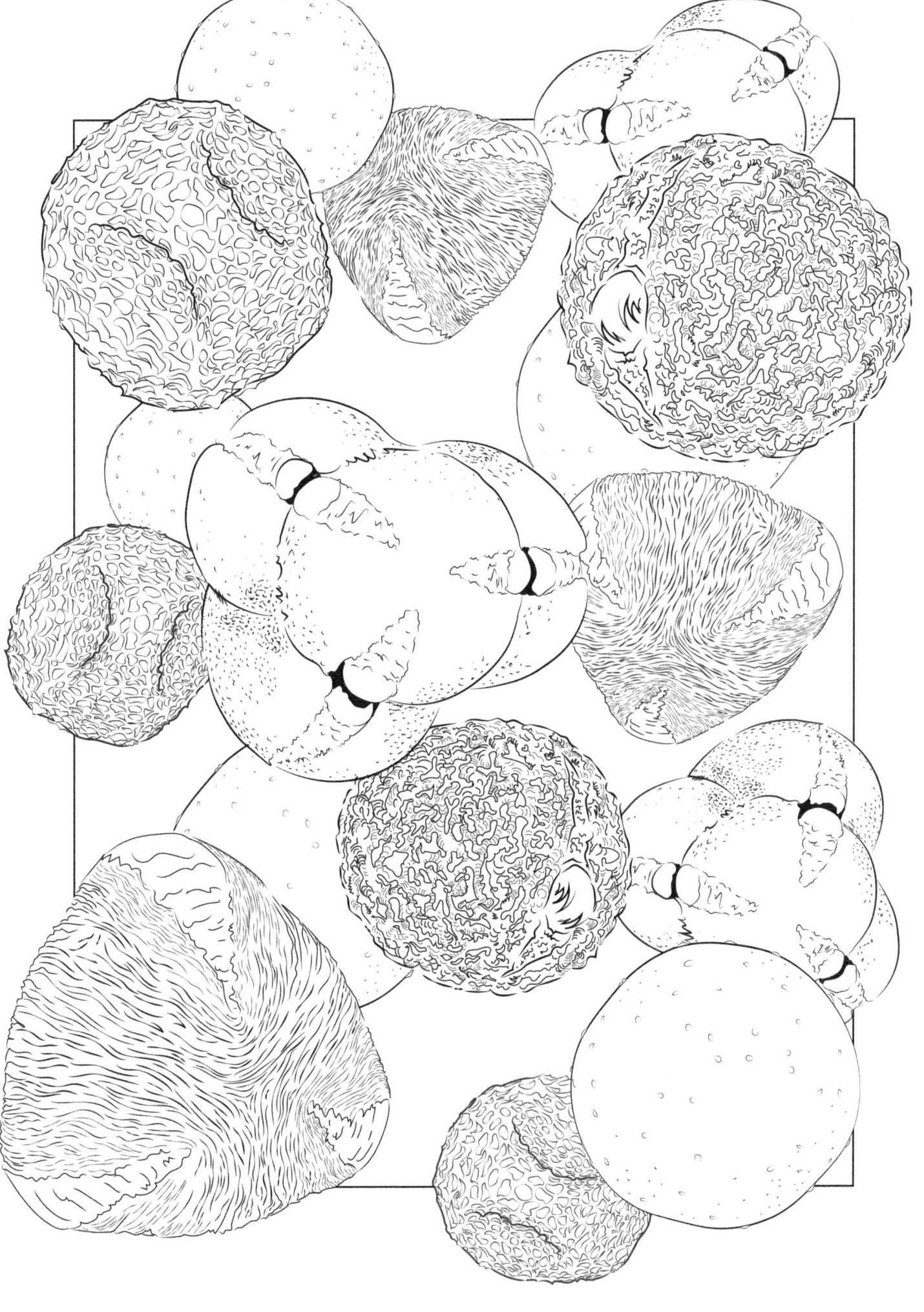

Under the sea
Cordelia Norris, illustrator

Until recently, scientists assumed that all underwater plants are pollinated by hydrophily, or pollen transport by currents and tides. New research has uncovered previously unknown connections between some very tiny sea animals and seagrass pollination.

Sea grasses grow on ocean bottoms in coastal regions around the world, forming underwater meadows that provide vital habitat across the food web, from the smallest marine organisms to charismatic megafauna, like **green sea turtles (Chelonia mydas)** and manatees. One type of seagrass, **turtle grass (Thalassia testudinum),** found in the Caribbean Sea and the Gulf of Mexico, is dioecious, with separate male and female flowers. Male turtle grass flowers release mucilage at night when small invertebrates like bristle worms and tiny amphipod crustaceans are active and hungry. This nutritious and carbohydrate-rich food also contains pollen.

Through carefully controlled studies, we now know that these invertebrates or "sea bees" visit the flowers, feed on the pollen and transfer it to the stigmas of female flowers, similar to the way that bees and other animals pollinate plants on land. A team of researchers from the National Autonomous University of Mexico, led by marine biologist Brigitta van Tussenbroek, coined the term "zoobenthophilous pollination" to describe this process.

This exciting find has opened the door to new research in the pollination of other sea plants. Understanding the reproduction of seagrasses is especially important because of their role in providing food and habitat, as well as storing carbon and protecting coasts by anchoring sediment with their roots.

Wandering lover
Tiffany Miller Russell, illustrator

Perfectly camouflaged among the petals, a female **white-banded crab spider** *(Misumenoides formosipes)* lies in wait to make a meal of a visiting pollinator. Her stripes, knees, toes, and eyes are usually rose-pink but can range from black to leaf green to dark yellow. She can change her main body color between yellow and white, matching the hue of her home flower.

The tiny male is 20 to 50 times smaller than the female, about the size of one of the dots on her back. He does not change color. His two pairs of front legs are even more extreme in size than hers, and are dark red, almost black. His body and two back leg pairs are bright olive green or toffee brown, and his abdomen can be yellow to bright red.

While the female waits to snag a bee or butterfly, the male searches for female spiders by jumping from flower to flower. He can't afford to stop and wait for a meal and rarely acts as a predator, instead taking his meals as he moves. He drinks nectar to feed and hydrate his small body. While doing so, he carries pollen from one flower to the next.

Crab spiders can be found almost anywhere in the garden and wilds, but they favor flowers such as chrysanthemums, wild carrot, rudbeckias, and **white snakeroot** *(Ageratina altissima),* a common wildflower native to eastern North America. This tall plant has tiny brilliant white flowers with plain green foliage.

Snakeroot is extremely poisonous and is responsible for the deaths of thousands of settlers in the early 19th century. "Milk sickness" is a fatal disease caused by the build-up of toxins from consuming milk and meat from cows that browsed on white snakeroot. One of the victims includes Abraham Lincoln's mother, Nancy Hanks Lincoln, who died when the future president was only nine years old.

A world in miniature

Chelsea Housand, illustrator

Minute pirate bugs *(Orius insidiosus)* are one of only a few true bugs (suborder Heteroptera) that pollinate plants. Bugs are identified by a unique type of forewing and sucking mouthparts. They are usually either predators or plant pests.

At ⅛ inch (3 mm) or smaller, pirate bugs are tiny omnivorous predators that are best seen with a hand lens. They have a painful defensive bite and hunt pests such as **thrips** (an ancient insect lineage that was one of the first pollinators of early flowers) as well as aphids, spider mites, and whiteflies. These important predators are used as beneficial bio-controls in gardens and commercial crops.

Moving between flowers in search of prey, they carry pollen with them. Pirate bugs also eat pollen and drink sap when prey is scarce. Minute pirate bugs shine like tiny gems with a pale bronzy-gold band across the outer wings, offset by the bug's black body.

Leafy spurge *(Euphorbia esula)* is a lush-looking invasive plant from Eurasia. The cup-like leaves surrounding the inflorescence are a neon-greenish yellow that contrast the plant's blue-green foliage. Euphorbia is a large genus of plants that grows worldwide. While the forms are very diverse, they all have a unique flower structure called a cyathium, which is actually the head of several tiny flowers that have been reduced to their most basic function. Each flower is either male or female and completely petalless. Surrounding this cluster, brightly colored and highly modified bracts have fused and taken the place of nectary glands. Nearby leaves take the place of showy petals.

Some thrips are so small that they suck juices from a single plant cell.

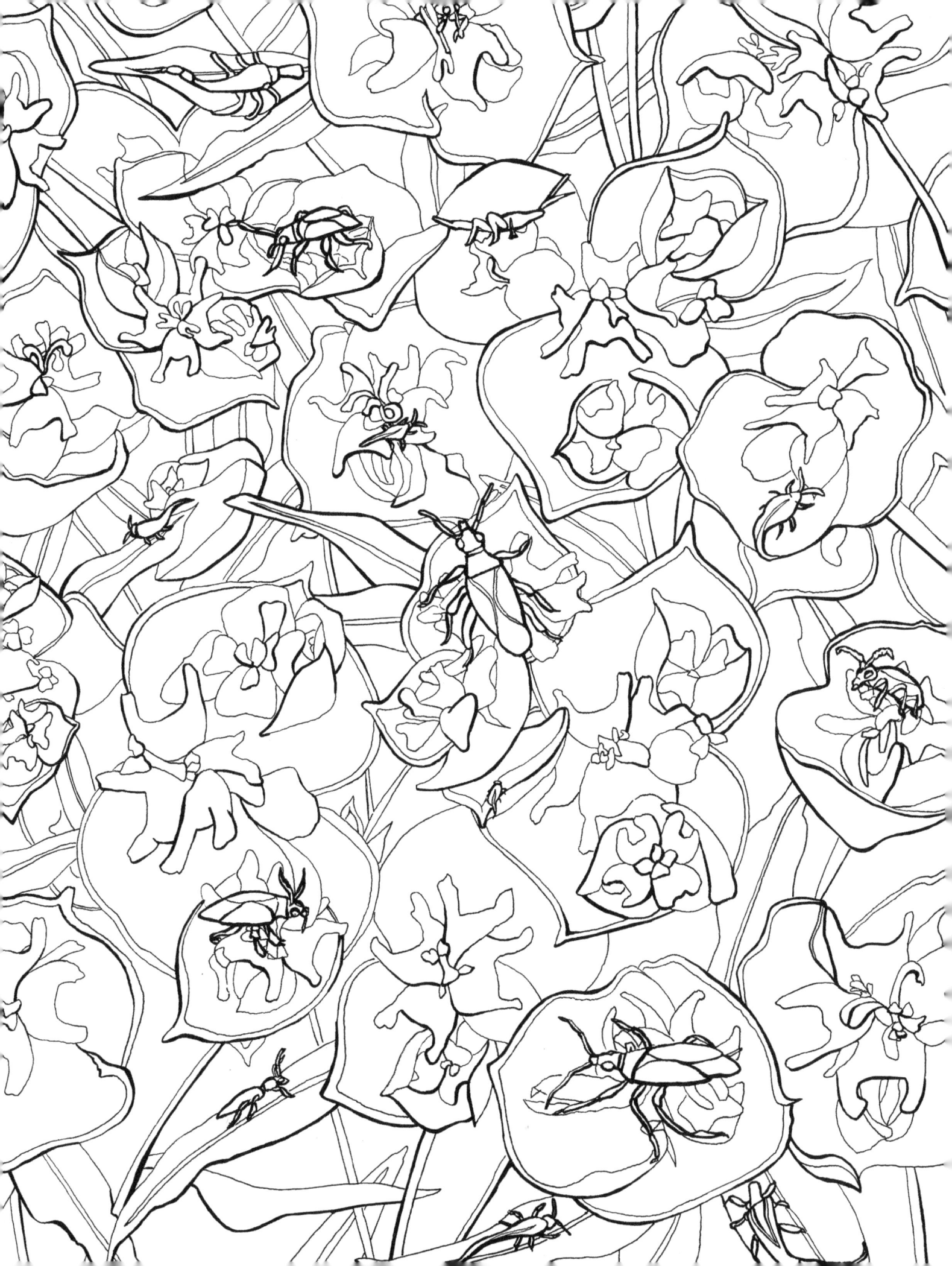

Swimming in snow melt

Taina Litwak, illustrator

Blunt-leaved orchids *(Platanthera obtusata)* are found in more northern climes worldwide. In North America, their range includes much of New England and the Great Lakes region, as well the Rocky Mountain states and the Pacific Northwest. The tiny ⅛ to ¼ inch (3-7 cm) greenish flowers grow along a single stalk and bloom in mid-summer. The flowers have pollinia or pollen balls with thousands to millions of compacted grains. The fragrant flowers attract small moths, bees, and snow pool mosquitoes. The pollinium becomes attached to the insect's eyes and sticks to the stigma of the next orchid.

Snow-pool mosquitos *(Aedes communis)* are the earliest mosquitoes to appear each year. Their larvae are found in snow pools in the same areas where the blunt-leaved orchids grow. Snow pool mosquitoes drink the nectar in the blunt-leaved orchid's tiny spur. Carlyle Luer, a scientist studying native orchids, observed that the mosquitos looked like they were wearing headlamps as they swarmed around the orchids with yellow balls of pollen on their faces.

Mosquitoes eat nectar as a basic food, but the females also need protein in the form of blood so that their eggs can develop. Humans have thin skin and less hair than many other animals, making us an appealing quick bite to the expectant mothers. Otherwise, nectar is enough.

Female snow pool mosquitoes lay their eggs above the waterline in damp soil near a river or lake. The presence of bacteria in the pools of water lowers the oxygen levels and triggers the larvae to hatch. Without this trigger, the eggs can survive for several years and will be ready to hatch the next time the water rises.

Lured and trapped

Jennifer Deutscher, illustrator

Just about every discussion of **fungus gnats** (families Mycetophilidae and Sciaridae) begins with steps for getting rid of them. While they may be pests on indoor plants, they're effective pollinators of many outdoor plants including the **Jack-in-the-pulpit (Arisaema triphyllum),** a job which often costs them their lives. At just hundredths of an inch long, fungus gnats are smaller than an eyelash and are weak flyers, which we experience when they fly into our faces and eyes.

Jack-in-the-pulpit flowers are easy to spot because of their unusual shape. The flowers are green with purplish brown stripes. The big leaf, called a spathe, forms the pulpit, with a greenish yellow spadix or rod inside, which carries many tiny flowers. The plants are dioecious, meaning that the spadix will carry either all male or all female flowers. The male flowers have four stamens filled with pollen. The female flowers have a fuzzy stigma on top of the ovary.

Attracted to their fungal scent, gnats visit the flowers to lay their eggs. Once the gnats realize there are no fungi, they try to exit the flower, only to find that it's so slippery that they can't get out. They keep trying and if the plant is a male, they find a little slit at the bottom and escape covered in pollen. If the plant is a female, there is no opening and the gnat dies within it. The maturing fruit of a Jack-in-the-pulpit often has entombed gnats inside.

Jack-in-the-pulpits can change the sex of their flowers from one season to the next. Female flowers require more resources to support flowering and fruit, supplied by starches stored in the plant's corm, or underground stem.

Fuzzy flies

Carol Schwartz, illustrator

With its black and tawny yellow coloring and its buzzing sound, the **bee fly** *(Villa lateralis)* resembles a bee, but it is in the fly family. It has two almost transparent wings, large eyes, long legs, and short antennae. Bee flies emerge in early spring and their furry bodies help them to keep warm and pick up pollen grains as they visit flowers. With the ability to hover in midair, darting back and forth and easily changing directions, they can visit many flowers in a short time, making them better pollinators than bees.

Bee flies have long proboscises that allow them to access the nectar of plants such as the **Virginia spring beauty** *(Claytonia virginica)* while hovering. In the process, a few pollen grains stick to their coat and travel to the next flower. Bee flies are considered to be even better pollinators than bees, perhaps because of their ability to move quickly from flower to flower.

The Virginia spring beauty blooms from April to June and its early flowering benefits many pollinators. The five star-like pale pink petals with darker pink veins and deep pink-tipped stamens grow on a small woodland plant that's six to ten inches (15-25 cm) tall. The flowers bend their heads and close up at night and on cloudy days, and open to greet pollinators on sunny days.

Bee flies hover over the ground searching for nectar as well as nests that female bees have worked hard to provide with pollen to feed their young. While the female bee is foraging, the bee fly lays her own eggs in the unprotected nest. The bee fly larvae feed on the provisions and developing bees.

Generating heat, wind, and odor
Carol Creech, illustrator

Eastern skunk cabbage (Symplocarpus foetidus) certainly lives up to its name. It's skunk-like odor both deters herbivores and attracts pollinating fly species such as the orange-eyed metallic **blue bottle fly (Calliphora vomitoria)**. The plant's rotting-meat scent attracts flies, lured by the prospect of a meal and a place to lay their eggs.

Skunk cabbage grows in wetlands and is one of the first flowers to emerge from the ground, not even waiting for the snow and ice to clear. This plant utilizes thermogenesis, creating its own heat through a chemical reaction. This allows the inflorescence to melt through the frozen mud and take advantage of the early spring insects. The warmth spreads the scent through the air, advertising a cozy place to stay and a meal of rotting meat. The inflorescence even mimics the look of the fly's meal. The large enclosing bract, called a spathe, is a deep maroon or burgundy color, flecked with yellow. The yellow flowers inside are arranged on a structure called a spadix.

The heat the skunk cabbage creates works with the asymmetry of its spathe to set up an internal 'cyclonic vortex' of air movement. The directional flow brings pollen in and spirals it directly onto the flowers while fanning the scent outward to reach its pollinators.

Despite being known for their unsavory food preferences, bottle flies are excellent pollinators. They fly in cooler, shadier weather than bees, and many woodland plants are pollinated by flies. They're most attracted to pale purple and brown flowers with a strong carrion scent and the nectar of these flowers is a favored source of nutrition. Working together to find food, flies release a pheromone in the air alerting others of the food source. Communal egg laying works to their benefit, too. Greater numbers of larvae produce more enzymes that help break down the carcass and make it easier to digest and their joint body heat helps keep all the larvae warm.

Siren scent

Deborah Shaw, illustrator

Certain plants and pollinators have special relationships, such as the black and yellow **bird hover fly** *(Eupeodes volucris)* and the **stream orchid** *(Epipactis gigantea)*. The stream orchid has evolved to produce a scent that's irresistible to hoverflies.

The stream orchid is found from British Columbia through the western United States and into northern Mexico. While tropical orchids are epiphytes, growing on the sides of trees, temperate zone orchids, like the stream orchid, are terrestrial and grow in the ground. They depend on a symbiotic relationship with particular soil fungi, and don't transplant successfully. The stream orchid blooms from March throughout the summer in shorelines of streams, lakes, and marshes.

The variegated colors of these orchids defy easy descriptions: the yellowish green flowers are veined with red-purple; and the bright red-brown lip or labellum is cup-shaped with a pointed, tongue-like protuberance with yellow, purple, and orange markings.

Hoverflies are drawn to the stream orchid by a scent that mimics that of the sugary "honeydew" excreted by aphids. Hoverflies typically lay their eggs on groups of aphids, which the larvae use as a food source. Stream orchids mimic the honeydew scent, attracting pollinators like the flies and some wasps. The hoverfly lands on the front half of the lip to sip the scented nectar and is propelled to the rear half where it lays its eggs within the flower. As the fly leaves, it brushes against the stigma and the pollinia, picking up packets of pollen on their backs.

Stream orchids are also known as chatterbox orchids. When the flower is touched, the lower lip moves like a chatting tongue. Wild orchids are endangered and are best enjoyed with your camera or eyes.

Who likes flattops?

Taina Litwak, illustrator

The robust *Belvosia borealis,* a species of the **bristle fly** in the Tachnidae family, is a bit bigger than a bumblebee at ¾ of an inch (2 cm) long. The segments of its bright yellow abdomen are punctuated by bands of spiky black bristles, and its feet, or tarsi, are orange tipped. Its thorax, legs, and wings are black. Its white face features black eyes with an iridescent sheen of teal or burgundy.

Tachinid flies are found in most of North America, reaching their peak numbers between July and August. With their short tongues, they're good pollinators of small flowers, especially those with relatively flat tops like feverfew and others in the Asteraceae family.

Tachinid females lay their eggs on an insect host or inside the host's body. To hatch, the eggs must be inside a host, and, once they hatch into larvae, they will begin to consume it internally, keeping the host alive until they are mature enough to leave. Tachinids are useful in the garden because they parasitize beetle larvae such as Japanese beetles, invasive moths, and grasshoppers among others, eating their body tissue and vital organs but not killing their host.

Feverfew *(Tanacetum parthenium)* blooms from July to October in gardens, meadows, and fields throughout North America but are native to the Balkan Peninsula. They resemble chamomile flowers and are sometimes mistaken for them. They are composite flowers with both disk flowers and ray flowers. The florets are arranged in a flat-topped cluster, white at the outer edge and yellow in the interior. The name feverfew comes from the Latin word "febrifugia" (fever reducer) because the plant was used medicinally for fevers and other ailments.

Planting flowers like feverfew that attract tachinid flies can help to control many pest insects. Tachinids can survive at higher elevations where bees cannot, and areas without bees can benefit from their pollination.

Tiger-striped enchantment
Vicky Earle, illustrator

With a wingspan of four to five inches (10 to 12.5 cm) and four black stripes on its pale-yellow forewings, **western tiger swallowtails *(Papilio rutulus)*** are large and striking butterflies. The back edges of their wings are triangular with sword-like protrusions at the bottom of the hind wings, similar to the tail of a swallowtail bird. Their range covers much of western North America along the coast and into the interior. The related species, eastern tiger swallowtails, Papilio glaucus, are found east of this range and have an impressive six inch (15 cm) wingspan.

Western tiger swallowtails are seen in wooded areas, parks, and gardens, gliding through the air and landing on flowers like the lavender hued **Canada thistle *(Cirsium arvense),*** an invader from Eurasia. Male butterflies are just as likely to be seen "mud puddling," gathering together in and around mud and sipping the water. Wet sand or dirt are an important source of salts and other minerals. Gardeners can help them by leaving small open areas near their plantings for shallow butterfly puddles.

Western tiger swallowtails practice Batesian mimicry, where a harmless species has evolved to imitate a dangerous or distasteful species in order to deter predation. After several molts, the caterpillars turn bright green and have two forms of protection—large eyespots on their tail end, and a brightly colored and foul-smelling forked appendage that emerges behind the caterpillar's head when startled. This snake-like stinkhorn, or osmeterium, wards off predators like wasps and birds.

Nectar thieves

Carla Schmakel, illustrator

Silver-spotted skippers *(Epargyreus clarus)* are one of the largest and most numerous of the over 2,000 skipper species in the Americas. They're found from Northern Mexico to Southern Canada. They have large compound eyes that can see ultraviolet light and brownish wings with a prominent white spot on the hind wing that gives them their name. Other wing spots are orange. Like all skippers, they're fast fliers with a jerky flight pattern that helps them evade predators.

With a long proboscis, they can feed on a variety of flowers. They favor the nectar of daisy-like flowers in the Asteraceae family, such as such as the **gray-headed** or **yellow coneflower *(Ratibida pinnata)*** and lay their eggs on plants of the pea family, like the **white wild indigo *(Baptisia alba)*.** Silver-spotted skippers can be seen in fields, gardens, meadows, and woodland edges.

However, their daintiness makes them poor pollinators of some of their favorite flowers. Gray-headed coneflowers are actually a cluster of many specialized individual flowers. Known as ray flowers, they attract pollinators with a showy display. The central part of the flower head, the disc, contains the fertile flowers. Flowers in the male phase are concentrated in the center and female-phase flowers are located around the outer rim. The long legged silver-spotted skipper lands lightly on the flower, and concentrates its probing where the nectar rewards are greatest—in the male central part of the disc. The skipper gets covered in pollen but it mostly avoids the female flowers, resulting in successful pollination less than 50% of the time.

Skippers (family Hesperiidae) look very different than other butterflies in the super family Papilionoidea. Their antennae feature a sharp hook called an apiculus at the end of the clubbed tip. They have large eyes, are chubbier, and have smaller wings which they hold at different angles when at rest. They are strong and maneuverable fliers and can achieve speeds of up to 20 mph (32 kmh). At night, or when they aren't foraging, they perch upside down under leaves.

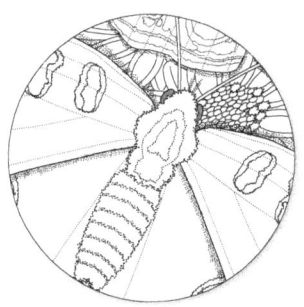

Changing with the seasons
C Olivia Carlisle, illustrator

Found in the United States, east of the Rocky Mountains, the **common buckeye (*Junonia coenia*)** rests on plants with its wings spread wide open, displaying large eyespots. In addition to scaring away predators, these large, multicolored eyespots trick predators to attack the hindwing instead of the more vulnerable head. Unlike some other butterflies, the common buckeye can survive an attack on its wings and function with up to two-thirds of its wings missing or tattered.

Common buckeyes look different in different seasons. They have roughly three generations a year. In the summer, the undersides of the wings are lighter in color to better blend with the lighter, brighter spring and summer colors. In autumn, the undersides are darker and browner to blend with the browns of fall. The upper sides of the wings are brown or blue, rimmed with orange and brown. In addition to the eyespots, white patches and orange distal bars combine to make this butterfly quite visually stunning, despite its small size.

Buckeyes have short proboscises and drink nectar from flowers with a short throat like the **chrysanthemum** (Chrysanthemum indicum)*. Some chrysanthemums have a compound called pyrethrum, which attacks the nervous system of insects. The mosquito and tick repellent permethrin is modeled after this natural compound. Planting chrysanthemums near other flowers discourages pests such as aphids, spider mites, and leafhoppers. Bees that visit chrysanthemum flowers have a greater resiliency to mites that infest their hive. Chrysanthemums are a great nectar source and bloom well into the fall.*

Good medicine

Amelia Svec, illustrator

One of the most widely distributed butterflies, the **painted lady** *(Vanessa cardui)* is found nearly worldwide, with the exception of Antarctica and South America. Painted ladies can fly as fast as 30 mph (48 kph) and cover 100 miles (160 km) in one day. In North America, they usually migrate in a northwestern direction during the spring. It takes about six generations for the many thousands of them to make their round-trip journey from Mexico to Canada and back.

Like many butterflies, they have different patterns on the underside and topside of their wings. The dorsal, or upper side, is orange with black and white markings. While the ventral, or underside, of the forewing shows a streak of red, most of the underwings are muted browns and tans. Butterflies typically land with their wings closed, showing the paler muted side, perhaps as a means of camouflage from predators. With their furry bodies, painted ladies are successful pollinators, feeding on many plants in their travels. In the process of feeding and breeding on sunflowers, they can damage the plant, a concern for farmers as well as bees.

Why bees? Research into the parasitic infections afflicting bee populations has found that bees that ingest **common sunflower** *(Helianthus annuus)* pollen have fewer infections. If they do get infections, sunflower pollen can help them recover. Since pollen is the single source of lipids and protein for bees, the nutritional quality of pollen is critical. Bumblebees, like the **common eastern bumblebee** *(Bombus impatiens),* from farms with more sunflowers have lower infection rates, so planting sunflowers appears to be a simple solution to help improve the health of bees.

When shopping for seeds, you may notice that some sunflower seed packets state that their variety lacks pollen. That means they have only female traits—pollen is a male characteristic. By choosing open-pollinated or heirloom seeds instead, you'll know that you're also helping the bees.

Golden skies

Amanda Surveski, illustrator

The iconic orange-gold and black **monarch butterflies** *(Danaus plexippus)* are known for their migrations, turning the sky golden as they fly in groups of hundreds of thousands. While well-studied, the migratory patterns of monarchs still contain mysteries. Monarchs west of the Rocky Mountains winter along the California coast and into Mexico, while the monarchs of central North America migrate thousands of miles to the Oyamel forests of central Mexico.

The migration patterns of monarchs on the eastern seaboard aren't as well understood. While some also travel to the forests of central Mexico, others go to the Yucatán Peninsula, Florida and the Caribbean. The monarchs that migrate to the south aren't the same as the monarchs that return, however. Three or four generations of monarchs are born and die along the journey, yet they find their way back to the same sites year after year.

It's critical that **milkweed** (*Asclepias* species) is available when the monarchs arrive in early summer. Monarchs co-evolved with plants in the milkweed family and depend on them to reproduce. Monarch butterflies lay their eggs on the underside of the leaves and the caterpillars rely on milkweed leaves for nourishment. The plant's toxic glycosides make both the caterpillars and butterflies unappetizing while making birds, lizards, and other animals sick. The growing caterpillars eat the leaves until they're ready to form a chrysalis, which turns transparent just as the butterfly is ready to emerge. Nectar from milkweed flowers also fuels the monarch migration flight, and the laying of eggs on milkweeds begins the cycle anew. Milkweed sustains monarch reproduction, and is an important nectar source for many other butterflies and bees.

Between climate change and changing land management activities, milkweed plants have suffered great losses. Planting milkweed now will make a real difference in the future, helping monarchs as well as other butterflies and bees thrive.

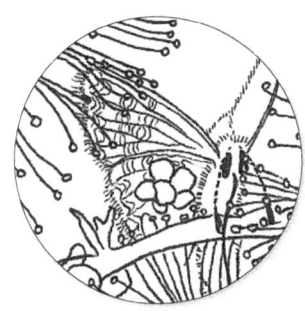

On gossamer wings

Karin Lakshmi von May, illustrator

The **marine blue butterfly** *(Leptotes marina)* is a member of the Lycaenid or gossamer-winged family. The upper sides of their wings are pale brown with a dusky iridescent-blue overlay that intensifies as the wings approach their fuzzy bodies. The undersides of the wings are patterned in broken waves of alternating ivory and camel, dotted at the hindwings with two inky-black eye spots.

A common butterfly, the marine blue is often found at the desert areas along the banks of waterways, and in parks and gardens throughout the southwest. It lives year-round in southern regions and is one of the few Lycaenids that has a regular long-distance migration. It migrates singly or in small groups, flying close to the ground in a rapid, jerky pattern. Its favorite plants are in the legume family, like wisteria, alfalfa, and the fairy duster.

Fairy dusters *(Calliandra eriophylla)* are small evergreen plants that are native to the southwest desert. They have lacy-looking blue-green, pinkish-stemmed foliage. The fluffy look of the flowers comes from their long pink stamens, rather than their petals, which are small and inconspicuous. Hummingbirds and butterflies feed on their abundant nectar. Their seed pods are dehiscent—when they reach maturity, they burst open and disperse the seeds by launching them.

The marine blue has expanded its range, taking advantage of urban gardens, and has been sighted as far north as Canada. Their caterpillars have a mutualistic partnership with ants. Like aphids, the caterpillars secrete honeydew, and are farmed and protected by ants. The Argentine ant is an invasive species that outcompetes native ants, but is particularly favorable to the caterpillars. This makes the marine blue one of the few species to benefit from humanity's influence on the ecosystem.

A healthy co-dependence
Taina Litwak, illustrator

The **yucca moth** *(Tegeticula synthetica)* and the plant that it pollinates, the **Joshua tree** *(Yucca brevifolia)* have evolved an obligate mutualism over the span of 40 million years, relying on each other for survival. In fact, when Joshua trees have been planted in other regions, extending to Ontario, Canada, the yucca moth follows the plants and pollinates them. The Joshua tree is native to the southwestern United States, particularly the Mojave Desert and the Joshua Tree National Park in California.

The small, light-colored yucca moth blends in well with the white blossoms of the Joshua tree. While the short-lived moths don't consume food as adults, the female moth gathers the sticky pollen from the anthers of male flowers under her chin. Visiting the flowers of a different Joshua tree, she checks for the presence of other yucca moth eggs, which she can smell with her sensitive antennae. If she finds no other eggs, she lays her eggs in the flower's ovaries and fertilizes the flower by rubbing a small amount of the pollen she's collected onto the flower's stigma. This act ensures that the flower will fruit and produce seed for her young.

It's said that the Joshua tree got its name from a group of Mormon settlers crossing the Mojave Desert in the late 1800s who felt they were guided westward by the trees. With its uplifted branches, these trees reminded them of the story of Joshua keeping his hands reaching up and out to guide the Israelites in their search for Canaan. Climate change poses a significant threat to the future of the species.

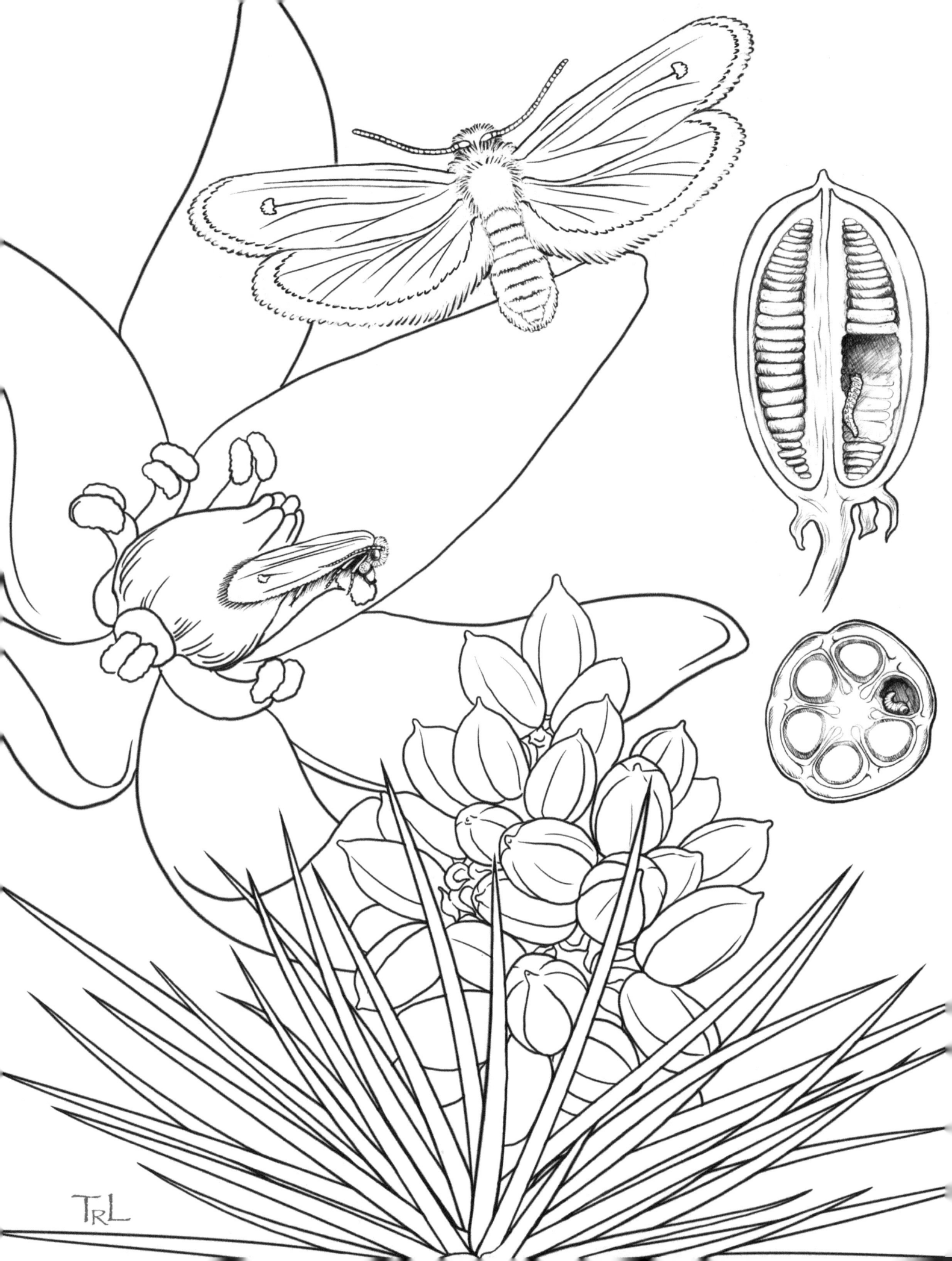

A one-day bloom

Maria Klos, illustrator

Among the muted browns common in most moth species, the **clouded crimson** is a standout. These vibrant moths have strawberry-and-cream colored wings, with a white abdomen and soft yellow thorax, and chartreuse green eyes. These bright colors actually help the moth blend in as they sit between the white and pink beeblossom flowers. Moths of the Schinia genus are known as flower moths and are often brightly colored. They share a strong relationship with their host plant, using its flowers and leaves as a food resource for all life stages of the moth.

Clouded crimson moths are in the family Noctuidae, the largest family in the order Lepidoptera, with more than 2,500 species in the United States and Canada. Moths in this family typically have hind wings and forewings that differ in color or pattern. Tympanal organs or ears located at the base of the hind wings help them detect and avoid bats and other predators.

The **scarlet beeblossom** or **scarlet gaura** *(Oenothera suffrutescens)* is named for its beauty, from the Greek word *gauros* ("superb"). The flowers occur on a spike-like inflorescence. Only one ring of flowers along its spike blooms at a time. The flowers change colors, opening white at night, turning to pink, and then to scarlet in the single day of the flower's bloom. The newly opened white flowers attract the night-flying moths who pollinate the plants.

Although clouded crimson moths are primarily nocturnal, they've been seen flying around blossoms of the Gaura species in late afternoon, a good reason to plant beeblossom.

The well-bred moth

Trudy Smoke, illustrator

The **garden tiger moth** *(Arctia caja)* is easy to identify by its deep brown forewings patterned with white. When opened, its hind wings are even more distinctive, featuring orange with dark dusky blue dots. The fuzzy thorax is brown and the abdomen is orange, continuing the color scheme of the wings.

Their conspicuous colors signal toxicity and help warn off birds. To protect themselves from bats, garden tiger moths audibly squeak and click to confuse their echolocation. Their conspicuous colors made them attractive to Victorian Era collectors in Europe, who bred the moths to create unusual patterning and forms.

As their name suggests, they visit gardens, meadows, woodlands, and sand dunes. Because of climate change, the garden tigers have moved further north in the United States, Canada, Europe, and cooler parts of Asia. Recent research into nocturnal pollination found that moths, including the tiger moth, carry pollen from a variety of plants, suggesting that the role of moths in pollination may be more important than was previously known.

The garden tiger moth caterpillars are called woolly bears. Furry and hairy, they emerge in late spring after wintering over. These black and orange caterpillars have a line of small white spots and like to bask in the sunlight and feed on stinging nettles, burdock leaves, and other garden plants.

In 1941 after a hunting trip with his dog, Swiss engineer George de Mestral looked closely at the burs sticking to his clothes and his dog's fur. The hook-and-loop structure of the burs of the **common burdock** *(Arctium minus) inspired him to invent Velcro. This invention, inspired by natural mechanisms, is an example of "bionics" or "biomimesis".*

Color-coded rewards

Samantha Gallagher, illustrator

The colors of the blooms that compose a flower cluster of the **common lantana (Lantana camara)** send a message to pollinators. The sequential color change of the lantana signals the availability of rewards. Central yellow flowers signal that they contain both nectar and pollen. Orange flowers signal that they contain smaller amounts, while the older red or magenta flowers around the outside of the cluster signal that they have no pollen or nectar.

Found in Florida and the coastal areas of the south, the striking **scarlet-bodied wasp moth (Cosmosoma myrodora)** has a bright red body, transparent wings edged and veined with black, and a metallic blue head and abdominal midline. The **polka-dot wasp moth (Syntomeida epilais),** also from Florida, is bluish black with white polka dots on the wings and body, and a red tipped abdomen.

Thrips, tiny insects of the order Thysanoptera, feed on plant saps, mites, and pollen. When consuming pollen, they cover themselves in a few dozen pollen grains and then groom themselves on the plant's stigma, leaving pollen behind, making them excellent pollinators.

Most wasp moths are diurnal or active during the day. These Batesian mimics are harmless but have evolved to look like stinging wasps to ward off birds and other predators.

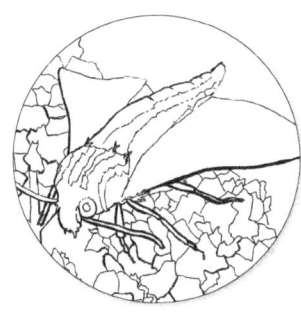

The misleading moth

Chelsea Housand, illustrator

Although the **titan sphinx moth** *(Aellopos titan)* ventures up to southern Canada, it makes the best use of its special coloration in South America. The titan sphinx has brown wings with white bars and a dark olive body with a pale underside. The short and thick dark brown abdomen has a bold white band at its base and a fan-like tuft of hairs at the tip. These colors resemble the patterns in tiny coquette and thorntail hummingbirds. The titan sphinx moths fly by day and visit the same flowers the hummingbirds do.

The moths' color pattern, quick movement, and strong hovering flight resemble female hummingbirds so closely that males perform courtship displays for them. Although the male quickly gives up displaying to the unresponsive moth, he will still aggressively defend his territory from other birds that present a threat to his nectar or his 'females'. This allows the moths to feed in peace, protected from predators.

In their northern range, the moths may find food at **red valerian** *(Centranthus ruber)*, an adaptable plant from the Mediterranean region that is a favorite in pollinator and xeriscape gardens. Titans and **white-lined sphinx moths** *(Hyles lineata)* as well as bees, butterflies, and hummingbirds find the scent and abundant nectar supply of red valerian irresistible. The flowers vary in color from deep wine red to light pink.

Jupiter's beard, another common name for red valerian, refers to Jupiter, who in Roman mythology was the king of the gods and the god of the sky and thunder. Images of Jupiter often show him with a tightly curled bushy beard, similar to the tight clusters of red flowers of the plant.

Darwin was right

Carrie Carlson, illustrator

With a whir of wings and a blush of brown and pink as it darts quickly from flower to flower, the **white-lined sphinx moth** *(Hyles lineata)* can easily be mistaken for a hummingbird. It has a large body and small wings which beat very fast, around forty beats per second, enabling it to hover as it feeds on nectar. One of the most abundant hawk moths in North America, these moths have excellent vision and are drawn to flowers by their color and nectar guides, the patterns or markings on the flower that lead the pollinator to the nectar. White-lined sphinx moths tend to be either diurnal (day active) or nocturnal (night active).

The **Rocky Mountain columbine** *(Aquilegia caerulea)*, the state flower of Colorado, grows in high, mountainous areas. The flowers vary from deep purplish blue to white, based on weather and location. The diurnal moths prefer the bluer flowers of the columbine, while the nocturnal ones prefer white colored flowers, which are more easily seen at night. The moth's long proboscis or tongue can reach into the long spurs of the columbine flowers to extract nectar, suggesting a co-evolution of the two species. Researchers are exploring the adaptive relationship between the color and number of the flowers produced each season, the weather, and the ratio of pollinating sphinx moths to bumblebees.

In 1862, Darwin hypothesized that the over 12 inch nectar spur of the star orchid of Madagascar signaled co-evolution between the flower and a pollinator with a long proboscis. More than 100 years later, he was proven right when a hawk moth with a proboscis more than twelve inches long was discovered in Madagascar.

Attack of the caterpillars

Megan Wilson, illustrator

The **tobacco hawk moth** *(Manduca sexta),* a gray moth with yellow-orange abdominal spots, and the white-flowered **coyote tobacco** *(Nicotiana attenuata)* have a mutualistic but antagonistic relationship. The nocturnal tobacco hawk moth relies on the plant's nectar and the coyote tobacco plant relies on the pollination of the moth for its survival, but this comes with a price for both the caterpillars and the plant.

The moths lay hundreds of eggs on the leaves which then hatch into caterpillars. Known as tobacco hornworms, the caterpillars start to eat the plant. The nicotine in the leaves doesn't bother the hungry caterpillars. To defend itself from being eaten, the plant releases volatile chemicals that react with the caterpillars' saliva, attracting bugs that then feed on the caterpillars. The plant also secretes a nectar which the caterpillars can't resist and, when they eat it, they start to smell like nectar themselves, attracting more predators.

The coyote tobacco plant's third defense is the most remarkable—the flowers switch from blooming at night to blooming during the day. This change attracts hummingbirds as pollinators instead of the moths. Once the caterpillars are no longer a threat, the plant switches back to blooming at night, again attracting the tobacco hawk moth, and so the cycle begins again.

The coyote tobacco plant has long been used for medicinal and ceremonial purposes by many Native Americans including the Hopi, Apache, Navajo, Paiute, and Zuni people. The greased and broken up leaves were also mixed with bearberry leaves to make tea.

The bountiful thistle

Amanda Surveski, illustrator

In a quiet spot in a summer garden, nature works cooperatively around a **field thistle** *(Cirsium discolor)*. Commonly seen as a weed, this native plant in the sunflower family is a valuable food source for many species including birds, butterflies, bees, and moths. The flowers are pinkish to purple and the underside of the leaves is whitish.

While a male and female **American goldfinch** *(Spinus tristis)* gather seeds, a **painted lady butterfly** *(Vanessa cardui)* seeks nectar. Nearby, a **snowberry clearwing moth** *(Hemaris diffinis)* sips nectar with its long proboscis.

With a black and yellow banded abdomen and tail-fan of black hairs, the snowberry clearwing moth could be mistaken for a large bumblebee. A black stripe runs through its eye, visually separating the top of the golden-olive head and thorax from its pale-yellow undersides. Its dark-margined wings are transparent. Unlike many other moths, the snowberry clearwing moth flies by day, hovering in the air as it sips nectar, and even hums like a tiny hummingbird.

Its caterpillars favor honeysuckle, dogbane, and the snowberry shrub and use their leaf litter to hide their cocoons. They emerge as adults with scale-covered wings, then gradually lose the scales to expose the clear membranes.

While goldfinches aren't pollinators, they perform a vital service for plants as seed dispersers. They're granivorous, eating seeds and gathering the fibrous thistle seeds to line their nests. Goldfinches are sexually dichromatic—in the spring the male is bright yellow with black patches and the female is a more muted yellow-brown. Both have orange beaks and are duller-colored after the winter molt.

The bees in the willows

Samantha Gallagher, illustrator

Dunning's miner bees *(Andrena dunningi)* belong to the Andrena genus, one of the largest bee genera in the world. They live in temperate climes and emerge when the ground is still cold and the plants they feed on have yet to blossom. To warm themselves, they rest in the sun until their internal temperature rises to at least 50°F (10°C), enabling them to fly.

Pussy willow trees *(Salix discolor)* begin flowering early in the spring, just as the hungry miner bees emerge from the ground. Both male and female miner bees pollinate the small trees as they gather pollen and nectar from the willow flowers. This relationship is critical to the survival of the willows and keeps the bees nourished until flowering crops such as apples, strawberries, and blueberries are ready for the miner bees to do their major pollination work.

Miner bees construct nests underground, visible as small holes in the dirt or leaf litter with small bees flying around. Miner bees are smaller than honeybees and are dark brown with pale bands of hair on their abdomen. They aren't aggressive and don't bite or sting. In addition to aerating soil, they also pollinate fruits that most of us enjoy.

Female miner bees dig their nests in loose ground and seal them with a waterproof, waxy substance. The primary chimney she creates has small offshoots where she plants balls of nutrients, lays an egg, then seals it off. The bee which hatches will spend most of its life underground until it metamorphosizes into a butterfly in a spring and leaves the nest to mate.

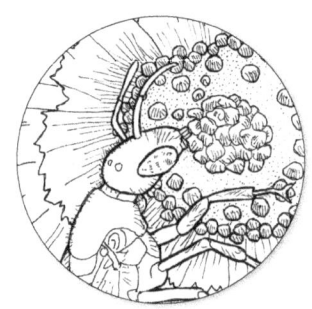

A delight of color

Susan Fox, illustrator

Visits to **large-flowered tickseed** *(Coreopsis grandiflora)* by **bicolored sweat bees** *(Agapostemon virescens)* create a blaze of orange, gold, and greens. The golden-yellow tickseed flowers have a dash of wine red at their petal's bases and a bright yellow or orange-gold center. The bicolored sweat bees are brilliantly colored, like tiny jewels. Their heads, thoraxes, and eyes are iridescent metallic green, and their legs are yellow. Males have bright yellow and black striped abdomens, while the females' abdomens are tawny and black, but sometimes metallic green as well.

Bicolored sweat bees nest communally under grass and leaves, but each bee is responsible for storing its own food. The males guard, protecting the burrow-like nests. Bees that have pollen are given priority entry into the nest, while those that have yet to leave are made to wait. They work together to restore the nest and keep entrances strong and safe from predators. Their lives are short, with multiple generations living over the course of a single summer, so it is important they keep their nests intact.

Sweat bees are important pollinators, pollinating a number of commercial fruit and berry crops such as watermelons, apples, blueberries, strawberries, and tomatoes, among others. They're polylactic, and feed on and pollinate a wide variety of flowering plantsfound in woodlands, fields, and gardens. A member of the Asteraceae family, the large-flowered tickseed is a favorite of pollinators because its shallow blossoms make it easy to get to the nectar and pollen.

These bees are called "sweat bees" because they are attracted to sweaty skin and sweaty people. They are generally nonaggressive and do not sting. They try to get close to people on a hot summer day for the salt and minerals that human sweat contains.

Sweeping up pollen

Erin Avery, illustrator

The **short leafcutter bee *(Megachile brevis)*** embodies the expression, "busy as a bee". These tiny ⅓ to ½ inch (1-1.5 cm) bees are solitary, living alone and not in hives. Leafcutter bees lay their eggs in "bee loaves" which provide both protection and nutrients to the encysted egg and eventual larva. The loaf is made out of pollen and nectar, and her saliva binds it together. She does this for each egg until she fills the nest, at which point she walls them in until the larvae can chew their way out in the next spring. Once the nest is secured, she dies.

Leafcutter bees are great pollinators of both garden flowers and farm crops. In controlled environments, such as greenhouses, each leafcutter can do the work of twenty honey bees. The hairs on the underside of their abdomens, called scopa (Latin for broom) turn yellow or orange when bees are carrying pollen. When not loaded down with pollen, the bees are mostly black, with pale yellow fur.

Up to four generations of these little bees may breed in a single summer. In the early fall, you may see them buzzing around the late season blooming **New England aster *(Symphyotrichum novae-angliae)***. These asters are found on prairies, gardens, woodlands, and along streams throughout most of North America. They have deep violet to pink or white ray flowers with golden colored disc flowers in the center. Those golden centers are filled with nectar and pollen, just what the leafcutter bee needs for her nest at a time when many other flowers have stopped blooming.

Leaf-stuffed crevices in walls, hollow plant stems, or dead trees, and small round holes in the leaves of your plants—these are both indication of the Megachile bee. The perfectly round holes that Megachile bees chew into leaves have been found in plant fossils dating over 30 million years ago.

The body language of bees

Cass Graybeal Brown, illustrator

Eusocial bees, like the **European honey bee** *(Apis mellifera),* live in a strict caste system, with male drones, non-reproductive female worker bees, and the reproductive queen bee, who produces up to 1,500 eggs a day. These highly structured colonies are considered superorganisms. Each bee has a particular function, assigned both by sex and by age. Honeybees can be considered to reproduce collectively, as colonies, as opposed to individuals.

The young female worker bees tend to the eggs and larvae; the middle-aged ones build wax combs, keep things clean, and guard the colony entrance; and the oldest ones gather pollen in their corbicula, a pollen basket on their hindlegs, and bring it back to the colony. Because of this, they are the most visible honey bees.

Bees communicate via pheromones, odors, vibrating their wing muscles while the wings are folded, and several types of dances. Foraging workers returning to the hive communicate to their sisters by performing what is known as a "waggle dance." Performed in a figure-eight pattern, the bee alters the orientation, speed, and duration of the dance. Through her pheromones and movements, she's able to tell the other hive workers the direction, distance, and the quality of the food resource. Other dances, called the "shake dance" and the "tremble dance" can recruit more workers for different tasks.

The **American white water lily** **(Nymphaea odorata)** *exists in a different stage of fertility each day, preventing the flowers from self-pollinating. During the first day, the petals don't open fully, but the plant produces fragrant nectar, attracting bees, flies, and beetles. When they land, they slip down the petals into the liquid in the bottom of the cup-shaped flower. If they have pollen, it's washed off and settles onto the receptive stigma below while the insect struggles to get out. On the second and third day, the flowers open and produce pollen. On the fourth day, the flower submerges so that the seeds can develop.*

A link to the divine

Aissa Domingo, illustrator

Stingless bees of the tribe Meliponini are found worldwide in tropical and subtropical habitats. Their stingers are too small to be useful as a weapon, so the bees defending the hive have a powerful bite. Despite this, only a few species of stingless bees are known to be aggressive.

Hive colonies are smaller (from a few hundred to a few thousand bees) than European honey bees (with colonies up to 80,000 individuals) and less practical for large scale honey production. Their honey is said to have a tastier flavor, more floral and less sweet than that of their European counterparts. Due to their small, easy-to-care for hives and more docile nature, many people in the tropics have hives of stingless bees in homes and urban apartments.

Royal lady bees *(Melipona beecheii)* are black with golden blonde hair on most of their body. According to Mayan history, they are the embodiment of a link to the spirit world. Greatly revered by Yucatec Mayan culture, they were valued both for both their honey and their wax, which was used for casting in jewelry making and metalsmithing. Hives would be kept in hollow logs near psychotropic plants such as the white-flowered **Christmas vine** *(Ipomoea corymbosa)* and the balché tree. The honey would take on the psychoactive properties of the bees' favored plants, and priests would harvest the honey in religious ceremonies. The tradition of keeping royal bees is still kept alive in those regions today.

Charles Darwin was fascinated by the fact that the honeycombs of melipona beecheii aren't hexagonal, but round. He hypothesized that the round cells represented an intermediary evolutionary step from bees that don't produce honey to the ones that do.

Unlocking hidden treasure

Alison Burke, illustrator

In 2017, the United States Fish and Wildlife Service added the first bumblebee to the endangered species list: the **rusty patched bumblebee** *(Bombus affinis).* The bumblebees are furry, with black hair that covers their heads, much of their legs, and the bottoms of their abdomens. They have golden yellow hair on the tops of their bodies except for a small rusty patch near their abdomen.

Once widespread in the East and upper Midwest, they are limited to a bit over a tenth of their initial territory. The rusty patched bumblebees are an important pollinator of wildflowers, like **goldenrods** of the *Solidago* species, as well as food crops like cranberries, plums, apples, alfalfa, peppers, and tomatoes. Their decline could have far-reaching effects on ecosystems.

The bees are active from spring to fall, and, unlike many other bumblebees, they can fly in cooler temperatures and lower light. They require flowers that bloom well into the fall, like goldenrod, which is native to most of North America with different regional varieties. Each flower head consists of many yellow ray and disc florets. The rusty patched bumblebee and other bees collect goldenrod nectar, which some bees use to provision their nests. While goldenrod has an unearned reputation for causing fall allergies, ragweed is the real culprit.

Rusty patched bumblebees "buzz pollinate". The bumblebee bites down on the flower's anthers while using her wing muscles to vibrate her whole body, creating a high pitched buzz and shaking loose tightly packed pollen. Some New World fruits, like tomatoes and peppers, as well as other fruits, like cranberries, require buzz pollination and only a few types of pollinators have this ability. You can help protect these essential pollinators by avoiding pesticides, planting goldenrod, and protecting native and natural habitats.

Up in the clouds
Carrie Carlson, illustrator

The subalpine ecosystem, just below the highest altitude at which trees are found to occur, varies widely from place to place. In Colorado's Rocky Mountain National Park, this is between 9,000 (2.7 km) and 11,000 feet (3.3 km), in Washington's Olympic National Park, this is between 5,000 (1.5 km) and 6,000 feet (1.8 km). In Denali, the subalpine zone lies below 3,500 feet (1 km) and in areas of western Alaska, there is no subalpine zone, as the treeline is at sea level. A treeline is not an actual line, but instead is the transition zone where trees get smaller and more stunted. In the summer, these areas can bloom with fields of wildflowers.

Colonies of **subalpine larkspur *(Delphinium barbeyi)*** thrive in these wildflower fields. Native to the interior western United States, subalpine larkspur has deep-blue to purple flowers and reaches heights of three to six feet (.9-1.8 m). The name delphinium refers to the flower buds that resemble jumping dolphins. The name larkspur describes the flower's long projectile that looks like the spur on the legs of some birds. Subalpine larkspurs can live over 75 years, and prefers moist, subalpine areas near streams or meadows.

Bumblebees, hummingbirds, moths, and flies forage for nectar in the flower's spurs. The spurs of the top two petals are hidden inside the larger spur on the upper sepal, forcing pollinators to probe deep inside for nectar. The **white-shouldered bumblebee *(Bombus appositus)*** favors the nectar of subalpine larkspur and is also one of the plant's main pollinators. These bumblebees are a bit larger, with bright white shoulders and a black band between the wings and a golden-yellow colored abdomen.

Delphiniums are poisonous to most mammals and cost ranchers millions of dollars in lost cows and horses. Unlike most livestock, sheep can eat larkspur, so many ranchers release their sheep into the fields first, and then later let out their cows and horses to forage on other plants.

False advertising

Mattias Lanas, illustrator

The magenta **pink lady's slipper orchid *(Cypripedium acaule)*** blooms from June to July. This beautiful wild orchid needs bees for pollination, and the **half-black bumblebee *(Bombus vagans)*** is one of the bee species that it attracts. Unlike most bumblebees, half-black bumblebees forage in forested and shaded areas, as well as meadows, roadsides, gardens, and wetlands. They have black lower bodies and a fuzzy yellow head. Males have some black on them, while females are mostly black with some yellow. These ground nesters build colonies with one queen and up to 70 female workers.

The orchids attract foraging bees with their bright pink color and sweet scent, which promises nectar. The bee climbs through a narrow opening at the bottom of the flower pouch expecting nectar, but soon finds there is none. In order to leave through one of two openings, the bee has to climb through the opening of the flower pouch, touching the hairs on it, where it picks up fresh pollen while depositing existing pollen packets. Although the orchid saves energy by not producing nectar, this deception strategy is less successful as, over time, the bees soon stop pollinating these orchids.

A pink lady's slipper seeds need to interact with a Rhizoctonia fungus in the soil. The mycelial threads of the fungus open the seeds and feed them. Upon maturing, the plant produces food for itself and the fungus as well, which it feeds through its roots. When two or more organisms evolve to support each other, it is called "symbiosis". Many terrestrial orchid species share similar symbiotic relationships with fungi.

Planting for the future
Sami Hernandez, illustrator

Once common across 21 U.S. states and seven Canadian provinces, **yellow-banded bumblebees** *(Bombus terricola)* are in serious decline and haven't been seen since 1999 in many of the states where they were once commonly found. These medium-sized bumblebees have yellow and black abdomens. The hair on the female's head is entirely black, while the hair on the male's head is pale yellow.

Researchers studying bumblebee decline cite commercial bee raising as a possible cause. Two species commercially reared to pollinate food crops were shipped back and forth between European facilities and those in the United States. It's theorized that the bees acquired a disease from the European bees. With no resistance to this new disease, the North American bees brought it back to the states and passed it on to wild bee populations. This is still being studied but the timing of the yellow-banded bumblebees' rapid decline supports this theory.

We can help boost bee populations by planting gardens that provide bumblebees with nectar and pollen. The **obedient plant**, or **false dragonhead** *(Physostegia virginiana)* is a good choice. Like all plants in the Lamiaceae mint family, it produces large amounts of nectar. White, pink, or lavender tubular flowers open along four foot (1.2 m) tall spikes. The five-lobed flower blooms in late summer and into the fall, providing bees with nectar for the coming winter months. Two are hood-like and form the upper lip, and three form the lower lip with the larger central one acting as a landing pad for insects, with bumblebees as the primary pollinators.

The obedient plant got its name because if you bend the flowers, they tend to stay in that position. Some gardeners swivel them into desired positions and they remain there until moved again.

Intensely active just above ground

Karin Lakshmi von May, illustrator

It's hard to spot the tiny **cactus bee** *(Diadasia rinconis)* hidden in the flowers and spikes of the **fishhook barrel cactus** *(Ferocactus wislizeni)*. Just ⅓ of an inch long (less than 1 cm), cactus bees are tawny with dark-banded abdomens. As solitary bees, they don't live in hives or have a caste system. Instead, they nest close together in large communities made up of thousands of bees where each plays a role. Male cactus bees patrol nesting sites, competing in "mating balls" for the chance to find a female partner.

Each female constructs and provisions her own ground nest by using nectar to soften the dry hard earth and then digs shallow vertical burrows of 10 to 12 cells. She then gathers nectar and pollen from cactus flowers to create a pollen loaf that she places in the burrows and lays her eggs on. Once finished, she seals up the nest, departs, and dies soon after. Her young will have food until they are ready to leave the nest.

The flowers at the top of the fishhook barrel cactus range from vibrant yellows and oranges to reds. The flowers have no spines or scales, but the cactus itself has yellow-red curved spines that extend from bottom to top. Shaped like a barrel and up to 10 feet tall (3 m) and 3 feet (.9 m) across with vertical spiny ribs, the southwestern barrel cactus grows in Central Mexico, Baja California, and the deserts of the American southwest.

The deserts of the Southwest have the highest diversity of bee species in the world. Fishhook barrel cacti attract a range of visitors, including butterflies, flies, ants, and European honey bees, but only cactus bees serve as pollinators.

Invader in the nest

Courtney Werner, illustrator

The flat-topped umbel of the wild carrot or **Queen Anne's lace** *(Daucus carota)* is made up of many tiny lacy white flowers with a single purple floret just off center. Queen Anne's lace attracts a variety of pollinators, such as the wasp and bee-mimicking hoverflies **Virginia flower fly** *(Milesia virginiensis)*, an amber, black, and yellow striped hoverfly, and the **American hoverfly** *(Eupeodes americanus)*, a yellow and black fly with burgundy eyes and a rim of fuzz around its olive thorax.

The **wild carrot wasps** *(Gasteruption assectator)* have black bodies tinged with amber, and the female wasps have a long black ovipositor. Sometimes confused for a stinger, the ovipositor is the organ she uses to deposit her eggs. Carrot wasps are parasitoid wasps that lay their eggs in the nests of other solitary bee and wasp species. While adult carrot wasps eat the nectar of flowers of the carrot family, the larvae need protein, which they get from the parasitized nests. The female checks a potential bee or wasp nest for activity using her antennae, and then bores a hole into the nest with her ovipositor and deposits her egg. The carrot wasp larva consumes the food meant for the other egg and sometimes eats the other bee or wasp larva.

The wild carrot flower or Queen Anne's lace is an introduced tall wildflower found in fields and meadows. The plant resembles the deadly poison hemlock. While poison hemlock smells bad, wild carrot flowers smell like carrots and the stem of the wild carrot is hairy while the poison hemlock's stem is smooth with purple blotches.

The vegetarian wasp

Aissa Domingo, illustrator

Scott Valley phacelia *(Phacelia greenei)* grows in only one place in the world, in the Scott Valley region of the southern Klamath Mountains in northern California. Formerly mined for gold, this area has serpentine ground derived from igneous ultramafic rock which makes for poor soil.

The flowers bloom from April to June and are deep purple with white centers. Fresh plants have mauve stems with soft sage colored leaves fading into blood red stems and orange leaves as the growing season progresses. As an annual growing plant, pollination and seed set is especially important for the Scott Valley phacelia.

The **pollen wasp *(Pseudomasaris vespoides)*** favors Penstemon, but also visits Phacelia and Eriodictyon. Closely tied to these three plant genera, it pollinates many rare native plants throughout western and central North America. Unlike all other wasps in their subfamily, pollen wasps are vegetarians and only consume nectar and pollen. Their long proboscises aid in the search for nectar. Instead of gathering pollen on hair, like bees, these wasps collect pollen and nectar in a crop.

Their nests are made from mud or soil, often hidden in crevices or under rocks. Each nest has four to ten cells, and each sealed cell has an egg with a single loaf of pollen and nectar. The eggs hatch and the larvae eat their loaves before pupating and breaking out of the nest as adults.

Pollen wasps are yellow and black with amber wings, and resemble yellow jackets. They can be distinguished by their club-shaped antennae, which are short and black in the female and long and yellow in the male. Their nests are distinctly different as well. Pollen wasp nests are made of mud while yellow jacket nests are made of paper.

Grasshopper hunter

Carla Schmakel, illustrator

While the **great golden digger wasp** *(Sphex ichneumoneus)* looks intimidating, it's a beneficial insect for gardeners, aerating soil, pollinating flowers, and catching grasshoppers. This wasp species has a black body, eyes, antennae, and abdomen tip. The wings are transparent amber and black, while the legs and front of the abdomen are deep amber. The head and thorax are covered in fine golden hairs that are often dusted with pollen. As adults, these wasps rely on nectar and sap for their diet, and carry off pollen in the hairs on their heads and bodies. They are non-aggressive and unlikely to sting unless handled.

From May to August, the female great golden digger tracks and paralyzes crickets, grasshoppers, and katydids to provision up to five or six nests. Using her strong mandibles, she digs a main vertical tunnel four to six inches (10-15 cm) deep with smaller horizontal larval cells. She transports the paralyzed prey to the nest, where she places it head-first in a side tunnel, lays an egg on it, leaves, and repeats this process until all tunnels are full. After covering the entrance with dirt, she leaves the larvae to hatch and consume the still-alive hosts until the young wasps are ready to emerge.

The **coralberry bush** *(Symphoricarpos orbiculatus)* is attractive to wasps because of its many nectar-filled flowers. Found in woodlands, fields, and pastures, the shrub spreads over time through stem-like runners called stolons. In midsummer, it has bell-shaped pinkish white flowers clustering along the stems. In autumn, the bushes produce bright magenta berries that provide food for birds, squirrels, and deer.

The great golden digger wasp uses her antennae and mandible to hold the paralyzed prey and fly or walk it back to the tunnel. While in flight, birds like robins and tanagers can give chase and harass the wasp until she drops the insect, which they grab and eat.

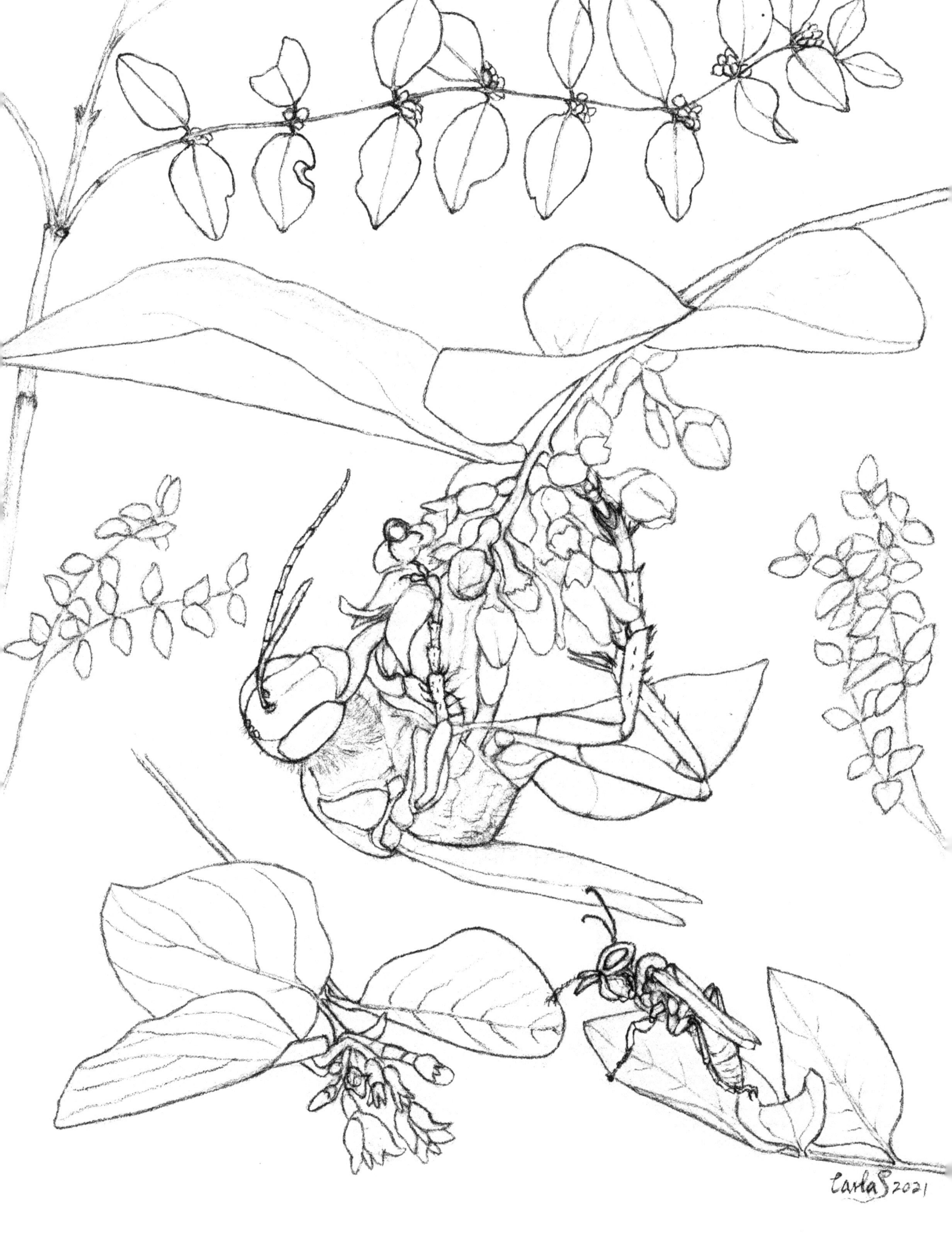

Perennially popular

Lauren Rosenfelt, illustrator

Wild bergamot *(Monarda fistulosa)* is a member of the beebalm genus, and is ideal for pollinators. The pinkish lavender flowers are a favorite of bees, wasps, butterflies, and hummingbirds. The flowers open continuously throughout the day, offering nectar as depleted flowers close and new ones open. This keeps pollinators foraging through the plants, looking for the best offerings. Young stigmas on newly opened beebalm flowers are less receptive to their own pollen, which helps prevent them from self-fertilizing. The steady stream of hungry pollinators ensures outcrossing and good genetic diversity in the next generation. Wild bergamot is found in prairies, savannas, and is used in many pollinator gardens.

The **great black wasp** *(Sphex pensylvanicus)* is a large, one inch (2.5 cm) long wasp with deep black wings that shimmer blue. Only the females have a paralyzing stinger. They belong to the digger wasp family. The female's nest is about a foot deep (30 cm) with multiple tunnels, each one supplied with a paralyzed grasshopper or katydid for her developing young. Adults drink nectar and are good pollinators of milkweeds and many other wildflowers.

The **common eastern bumblebee** *(Bombus impatiens)* is a major pollinator of native flora and is one of the most important bee species used in commercial greenhouses. The fur covering their body collects and traps pollen, which bees carry from one bloom to another. The bee is black-bodied with a fuzzy blonde thorax.

Wild bergamot is not only a pollinator's favorite, but is also known for its historical medicinal applications among native peoples. It's been used as a poultice for boils and cuts, as well as a tea for headaches, indigestion, colds, and the flu.

Dinner and a date
Lauren Rosenfelt, illustrator

Tall boneset *(Eupatorium altissimum)* is a plant in the Asteraceae family that has many sister Eupatorium species. Tall boneset's clusters of tubular white flowers are often covered with a variety of pollinators enjoying the plant's nectar, including **goldenrod soldier beetles** *(Chauliognathus pensylvanicus)*.

These colorful beetles are ½ inch (about 1 cm) long and are orangey yellow with two black bands on the base of their forewings (elytra) and thorax (middle section). Goldenrod soldier beetles feed on the nectar and pollen of late summer flowers, sometimes while mating. They're insectivores as well as nectivores and eat some of the insects we find troublesome, like aphids and caterpillars. For the beetles, tall boneset plants not only provide food but also a good place to meet, mate, and lay their eggs. Found in much of the United States, their population increases in late summer and early fall, just in time for the blooming of goldenrod and boneset.

Scientists studying tall boneset found that some populations are composed of mostly females, with only 10% of the plant's population producing viable pollen. Despite producing large quantities of nectar and attracting many flies, wasps, beetles, bees, and butterflies, these female plants are able to set seed on their own without ever achieving pollination. Each seed contains only the mother plant's DNA, and is a clone of the original plant.

Boneset, as its name implies, has been used medicinally in many cultures. Native Americans, European settlers, and enslaved Americans used it as a medicine for dengue fever (called break-bone fever in the South for the severe pain it caused) and flu-like symptoms. Valued for its anti-inflammatory properties, boneset was commonly brewed as a healing tea, although research suggests caution since some parts of the plant can be toxic to the liver.

The eater of insects

Claire Alderks Miller, illustrator

The carnivorous **Venus flytrap *(Dionaea muscipula)*** traps and digests insects using its foldable leaf, green on the outside and pinkish red on the inside, edged with tooth-like hairs. When an insect or an arachnid brushes against the trigger hairs twice, the leaf folds, trapping and digesting it. Venus flytraps are found only in the grassy wetlands within a 100-mile (160 km) radius of Wilmington, North Carolina.

The Venus flytrap's flowers rely on insects like bees and beetles for pollination, different species from their prey. The flowers, which are white with yellow anthers, bloom six inches (15 cm) or more above the leaf-traps. Their pollinators include sweat bees and beetles, like the **red-checkered beetle *(Trichodes apivorus),*** with its wing bands of alternating reddish orange and black, black legs, and fuzzy rusty black head. It also relies on the **notch-tipped flower longhorn beetle *(Typocerus sinuatus),*** with its yellow body, black disk-like spots on the side, and black head and legs. These beetles eat the flower's nectar, picking up pollen and avoiding the leaf traps. Insects like flies, spiders, and ants are not so lucky.

The **yellow pitcherplant *(Sarracenia flava)*** is also carnivorous and native to the coastal plains of Virginia and the Carolinas. It traps insects in its three foot (.9 m) high rolled leaf. The leaf has glands on its surface that secrete nectar and a waxy toxin that makes insects lose their footing and fall to the bottom of the flower. Once at the bottom, the flower's digestive fluid and spiky hairs make escape difficult. Research shows that Sarracenia flava bend their flowers at the right moment when in bloom to provide safe access to nectar and pollen, allowing for pollination.

Charles Darwin called the Venus flytrap the "most wonderful plant in the world," perhaps referring to its ability to trap food and still be pollinated.

From the earliest days
Bea Martin, illustrator

Before there were bees, butterflies, and moths, there were beetles and flies. Before flowering trees and plants were widespread, there were magnolias, considered to be among the first of the flowering plants. The relationship between beetles and magnolias began millions of years ago. While most trees are wind pollinated, magnolias evolved the then-novel strategy of producing scented flowers filled with nectar. Beetles and flies were their primary pollinators.

Four-spotted sap beetles *(Glischrochilus quadrisignatus)* are in the Nitidulidae family. Only about ¼ inch (.5 cm) long and oval-shaped, they are black with four orange-rust spots on their wing covers. They feed on decaying or over-ripe fruits and vegetables as well as sap. Their mandibles evolved to break off and chew vegetable matter, and they often eat the plants they derive nectar from. Perhaps because of this, magnolia flowers evolved to be tough, with thick white petals and well-protected seeds. Although sometimes referred to as "dumb" pollinators, sap beetles were critical to the survival of magnolias and still play an important role as pollinators.

Star magnolias *(Magnolia stellata)* grow to 15-20 feet (4.5-6 m) high and are popular trees in gardens and parks all over the United States. They are among the earliest plants to bloom, with three to four inch (7.5-10 cm) fragrant star-shaped white flowers. Magnolias produce lots of nectar, but less pollen than wind-pollinated trees. The stamens are arranged so that insects looking for nectar will bump into them and acquire and spread pollen. As the messy sap beetle finds nectar and moves the pollen along, it's maintaining a relationship that has lasted over 100 million years.

Most trees, like maples, oaks, and ashes, are wind-pollinated, and have tiny scentless flowers. This approach is successful because of the enormous number of anthers, the pollen-producing structures, producing huge amounts of wind-carried pollen.

An ancient pact

Tiffany Miller Russell, illustrator

Not all seed-bearing plants produce flowers. Gymnosperms or 'naked seeds,' includes conifers, gnetophytes, ginkgos, and cycads. Gymnosperms and their sister-group, the flowering angiosperms, both evolved from an extinct order of plants called the pteridosperms, or seed ferns. Most gymnosperms are pollinated by wind. Cycads are an exception that provide a window into one of the first mutualistic relationships between plants and animals. Fossil records of cycads date back to 280 million years ago, although today's living cycads evolved much later. Cycads are pollinated by thrips, moths, and beetles. Their pollinators are specialists, attracted only to their own favorite plant, and will ignore scents from other cycad species.

The **coontie *(Zamia integrifolia)*,** is pollinated by two beetles: a **cycad weevil *(Rhopalotria slossoni)*** and a **pleasing fungus beetle *(Pharaxonotha floridana)*.** Both beetles are the color of coffee with cream.

Each cycad plant is dioecious, either male or female. The male plants provide food in the form of pollen, a place to gather and mate, shelter, and a brood site for larvae. Female plants don't offer much in the way of rewards—their nectar has only weak concentrations of sugars and proteins and their seeds are too toxic to host eggs. The male plants push their pollinating visitors out. During midday, the male cones heat up, intensifying production of volatile chemicals. The same scents that usually attract beetles now reach unbearable levels and push them away, out toward the more mildly-scented female cone.

*The **atala butterfly** (**Eumaeus atala**) relies on the coontie to raise its red and yellow caterpillars. This pretty black butterfly with a red abdomen and iridescent blue spots was once thought to be extinct. Overharvesting led to the coontie becoming severely endangered in the wild. Now protected and encouraged as a garden planting in its native Florida range, both the coontie and the atala are making a comeback.*

The ultimate survivors

Bea Martin, illustrator

Hedge bindweed *(Calystegia sepium),* of the Convolvulaceae family, is found throughout most of the United States and Eurasia. It grows on twining vines and produces large buds and flowers that are funnel-shaped and two to three inches (5-8 cm) across with five lobes. The corollas are usually white although they can be pink or striped, and are yellow deep within the throats of the flowers.

Morning glory flowers are popular with pollinators and attract bees and moths, as well as a variety of beetles including the **red megacerus** *(Megacerus discoidus).* This tiny, .15 inch (3-4 mm) beetle's first pair of wings, called elytra, are orangey-red outlined in black, and it has a white body, with a black head, legs, eyes, and antennae. The megacerus's remarkable antennae help the beetle locate food and identify pheromones through receptors that provide information about touch, smell, and taste.

Cantharophily, or beetle pollination, is a messy process. Known as "mess and soil" pollinators, beetles eat their way through the flower petals. In their quest for pollen, they move from flower to flower, sometimes eating part of the flowers, sometimes defecating, and pollinating the plants.

Beetles that resemble their modern day descendants first appeared on earth about 230 million years ago. They've survived multiple extinction events that doomed many other animals, including non-avian dinosaurs and mammalian megafauna, but beetles adapted and thrived. Beetles pollinate more than 90% of flowering plants. With recent estimates of 1.5 million different types of beetles, they comprise about 25% of all described species on earth. Researchers estimate that approximately just 10% of the world's beetles have been named and described.

The beetle that purrs

Gabriela Sincich, illustrator

Red milkweed beetles are in the family of longhorn beetles, with long antennae set close to the eyes. In the red milkweed beetle, the antennal base divides each compound eye into two parts, resulting in a lower and upper eye (their Latin name, *Tetraopes tetrophthalmus,* means "four eyes"). They are red with black spots, black legs, and around ½ inch (1.3 cm) long. Males are smaller than females. Both sexes produce squeaking and purring sounds by rubbing structures on their thorax together. These vocalizations vary widely, depending on the situation, and may variously serve as alarms, love calls, or just friendly gossip.

Red milkweed beetles' lives center around milkweed plants, where they rest, feed, and mate. Adult beetles feed on the plant's foliage. They reduce their contact with its latex by opening up its veins. Since the latex can seal the beetle's mouth shut, the beetle must scrape it off immediately. They spend most of their lives on milkweed roots, hatching and growing from late summer until the subsequent spring.

Asclepias syriaca or **common milkweed** is a tall plant with ball-shaped umbels, or flower clusters, of sweet-scented pink to purplish flowers. Milkweed flowers have a unique structure for pollination. Rather than individual pollen grains, milkweed pollen is contained in pairs of small waxy sacs called pollinia that are located in stigmatic slits in the flowers. When the beetle visits the milkweed flower to get nectar, its leg or mouth parts may come in contact with the sticky pollinia which attach to the beetle. When it visits another flower, it transfers a pollinium to that flower.

Milkweed contains cardiac glycosides similar to digitalis used in treating heart disease. When absorbed by monarch butterfly larvae and milkweed beetles, the glycosides make the larvae and adult butterflies and beetles toxic to birds and other predators.

A sure sign of spring
Clara Hunt, illustrator

Baltimore orioles *(Icterus galbula)* are welcome visitors in the spring, not only because of their beauty but also their melodious song.

Oriole comes from "aureole", the Latin word for gold. With their bright golden orange body, black head, and black and white wing bars, adult male orioles are easy to identify. Immature males are more muted with paler golds and oranges. Female orioles are gray-green in color with grayish-white wing bars. Males are slightly larger than females.

In the early spring, Baltimore orioles leave their winter range and arrive in the central and eastern United States. Male and female orioles each play a role in parenting. Females build the nest and incubate the eggs, while the male feeds the female and protects the nest from predators. In the altricial stage, when the chicks have just hatched, both parents feed the babies and keep the nest clean. Once the young have fledged, the parents stay with them to forage for about a week. They then leave for their southbound migration, which can begin as soon as early July.

In their winter ranges, orioles are the primary pollinators of the **coral tree** *(Erythrina breviflora).* Many species of these tropical and subtropical trees have bright red flowers, which may be the source of their name. The nectar from these trees has enough sugar and essential amino acids for the orioles but isn't sweet enough to attract many hummingbirds, forging a co-dependent relationship between the orioles and the coral trees.

The state bird of Maryland, these orioles were named the "Baltimore Bird" in 1731 after the black and yellow shield in the coat of arms of the Calvert family, the colonial proprietors of Maryland.

Chasing the blooms

Susan Fox, illustrator

Hawai'i is home to many native flora and fauna that exist only there, including the Hawai'ian honeycreeper birds, 'apapane and 'amahiki. Hawai'ian honeycreepers are a specialized group of finches, evolving and diversifying in the isolation of the islands. Many eat insects, but they're mainly nectarivorous. Their tubular tongues have fringed tips, perfect for soaking up nectar. The **'apapane *(Himatione sanguinea)*** is bright red with black wing feathers and a black bill. The **'amahiki *(Chlorodrepanis virens)*** is yellow-green with a gray bill and black mask.

'Ōhi'a and koa trees are the two most common trees of Hawai'i, making them vital parts of the forest ecosystems. The **'ōhi'a lehua tree *(Metrosideros polymorpha)*** has large, fringe-like flower clusters made up of masses of long stamens. "Lehua" can refer to the tree or just to the flower cluster itself—the red flower is the official flower of the Big Island. The rare yellow flowers can pollinate themselves, but the more common red ones need external aid. The flowering **koa tree *(Acacia koa)*** has short flower stalks that grow pom-pom shaped masses of creamy-yellow flowers. In their search for nectar, birds fly long distances between the various islands of Hawai'i, following the blooming patterns of native trees. Many of Hawai'i's native bird species rely heavily on the nectar of 'ōhi'a and koa flowers.

Early Hawai'ians used koa trees to make single canoes with an outrigger (kaukahi), and double canoes (kaulua) made up of two canoes tied together with a special yoke. Highly valued for its tonal properties, koa wood is used to make ukuleles and acoustic guitars. Today, koa wood is one of the most expensive woods in the world.

The all-in-one cactus

Carol Schwartz, illustrator

White-winged doves *(Zenaida asiatica)* inhabit deserts and urban areas in the southwest, and their range is expanding. White-winged doves are brownish-gray with a bright white wing patch that expands into a white crescent in flight. Crimson colored eyes, blue eye rings, and bright pink legs and feet add striking splashes of color to their otherwise muted coloration. They eat fruit and seeds and will eat from bird feeders.

These doves are important pollinators, especially of the **saguaro cactus *(Carnegiea gigantea)*,** a large cactus native to the Sonoran Desert. Pollination is part of the mutualism between the cactus and the doves. The white-winged doves have evolved to synchronize their migration and breeding to match the flowering and seeding of the cactus. From April to June, hundreds of saguaro flowers bloom each day. The white, waxy flowers open after sunset and continue to produce nectar until they close the following afternoon.

Their flowers are self-incompatible and depend on cross-pollination from white-winged doves, honeybees, hummingbirds, and bats. Its many ovules require large amounts of pollen, which is produced by numerous stamens, in one case totaling 3,482 in a single flower. The doves also rely on that pollen and nectar for water and nourishment, and feed on the saguaro fruits and seeds. They regurgitate the seeds to their nestlings, and when seeds fall to the ground below, they're in an ideal growing spot.

The saguaro cactus is a keystone species, which means that other species in its ecosystem depend on it to provide food, shelter, and/or protection. In addition to the white-winged dove, Gila woodpeckers and gilded flickers nest by boring into the saguaros, and red-tailed hawks nest in crevices in the arms of the saguaro.

Feeding every few minutes

Sara Lynn Cramb, illustrator

At only three inches long (7.5 cm) and weighing 1/10 of an ounce (3 g), with jewel-toned iridescence, **Allen's hummingbirds** *(Selasphorus sasin)* are birds of extremes. They live in either a state of frenzied activity or in torpor. Owing to their high metabolism, hummingbirds need to eat over twice their weight in nectar each day. When at rest, they go into a torpor, allowing their body heat to escape and their heart rate to drop. In this state, they're still until the sunlight heats them enough to raise their body temperature and they can fly and feed.

During the warm months, Allen's hummingbird lives in a small strip of land along the Pacific coast in California and lower Oregon. In the cooler months, they migrate to central Mexico. This limited range increases their susceptibility to climate change, habitat destruction, disease, and natural disasters. Like most hummingbirds, they must feed at least four times an hour and may need to feed from up to a thousand flowers before their next torpor.

The male Allen's hummingbird has a fiery copper-red throat patch known as a gorget, and the female has a smaller gorget. The very top of their head and back is iridescent green, and their chests and bellies are white, but most of their feathers are reddish-brown. Their wing feathers are gray and their tails have black tips. They have long narrow bills, long tongues, and the ability to hover precisely in place. They're especially attracted to red trumpet-shaped flowers like the **red bush monkey flower** *(Diplacus puniceus)*.

The female hummingbird builds her nest in a tree before she mates. The nest is made of spiderwebs and parts of willows and flowers and is shaped by her body. The nests are tiny, measuring about just 1¼ inch (3 cm) across and 1½ inch tall (almost 4 cm). She lays two eggs and incubates them for close to three weeks. Once they hatch, she feeds them until they fledge.

Tiny muse

Charon Henning, illustrator

Named "Calliope" for the Greek Muse of poetry, song, and the arts, **Calliope hummingbirds** *(Selasphorus calliope)* are the smallest birds that breed in the United States. Just under three inches (7.5 cm) long, they weigh about $1/10$ of an ounce (3 g), about the same as a ping pong ball. They have short wings and tails that have a bit of rusty color at the base. The males have a bright magenta-streaked gorget and a creamy gray body. Their blackish gray bills are short for a hummingbird.

Calliope hummingbirds travel about 5,000 miles, from meadows in the foothills of the mountains of the Pacific Northwest to Mexico's pine-oak forests and back. This takes a year and they're the smallest birds to migrate such long distances

Calliope hummingbirds pollinate many of the plants they visit, particularly tubular-shaped red and orange flowers, like the **firecracker penstemon** *(Penstemon eatonii)*. This vivid plant is native to the western United States, from the high deserts of southern California to the Rocky Mountains. It grows in deserts, woodlands, forests, meadows, and gardens.

Through evolutionary adaptations, some flowers in the penstemon species have changed from being bee-pollinated to hummingbird-pollinated. The bee-adapted penstemon flowers exhibit traits designed to attract bees, including wide floral tubes, horizontal positioning, and a landing platform. The blue or purple flowers only produce small amounts of nectar. In contrast, the hummingbird-adapted penstemon flowers have narrow tubes, are bent downward, and have no landing platform. Bright red or magenta flowers signal large amounts of nectar to the hummingbirds. When flowers make adaptations to attract a certain type of pollinator, this is known as "pollination syndrome."

Night and day over the waves
Hannah Loeffelholz, illustrator

Ruby-throated hummingbirds *(Archilochus colubris)* are the only hummingbird species that nests east of the Mississippi. These tiny birds, which range to southern Canada, have remarkable endurance, flying non-stop across the Gulf of Mexico in the fall to their wintering ground, an approximately 20 hour flight. Ruby-throated hummingbirds are about three inches (7.5 cm) in length with a four inch (10 cm) wingspan, with males smaller than females. The males have brilliant iridescent ruby throats that may look black at certain angles. The females have creamy throats, while both males and females have dark green iridescent bodies and sides with creamy bellies. They have a small white spot behind their eyes and a black forked tail.

These little hummingbirds are the primary pollinators of 19 species and are important pollinators of at least a dozen others. They hover airborne while feeding, supported by wings beating about 80 times per second, and their tongue darts out every tenth of a second. They're attracted to the large nectar loads that red-orange flowers, such as those of the **trumpet vine** *(Campsis radicans),* offer. Hummingbirds are also insectivores and eat flying insects as they move from flower to flower.

The 4½ inch (11.5 cm) tube-shape trumpet vine flowers fit the hummingbird's bill perfectly and deliver a high-volume nectary of nourishment. Some birds, bees, and other insects also visit these flowers, but hummingbirds are ten times as efficient in acquiring and distributing pollen. Females and young hummingbirds tend to collect a heavy dusting of pollen on their heads. Bees, ants, and flies are also attracted to the sugary nectar, but the trumpet vines handle this by producing extrafloral nectaries in the petiole, calyx, corolla, and fruit.

Desert blooms

Charon Henning, illustrator

The **lucifer hummingbird** *(Calothorax lucifer)* is a sheartail hummingbird, with a deeply forked and narrow tail extending beyond the wingtips. Found in Mexico and the southwestern US, the lucifer hummingbird is about four inches (10 cm) from head to tail, and weighs under an ounce (less than 28 g). Like other hummingbirds, lucifers are sexually dimorphic. Females are bigger than the males, and the males are more brightly colored. Males have an iridescent green back and a light gray breast with a throat gorget that looks deep purplish black in dim light and bright purple in the sunlight. Females have a creamy breast and throat with cinnamon-colored patches on the underwing and iridescent green wings with a cinnamon patch on the upper tail feathers.

The down-curved bills of lucifer hummingbirds make them perfectly suited to gather nectar from the tube-like flowers of the ocotillo plant. **Ocotillos** *(Fouquieria splendens)* are not cacti, even though they have thorns and live in the desert. Spanish for "little torch," this desert shrub has fiery red flowers at the end of long spiny stems that can grow up to 20 feet (6 m) tall. Ocotillos are native to the Sonoran and Chihuahuan deserts in the southwestern United States and northern Mexico. Their early bloom, between February and mid-April, makes them an especially good food source for hummingbirds and carpenter bees.

Ocotillo plants, which can live up to 200 years, are a drought deciduous species and have evolved the ability to sustain themselves in severe droughts. When there's enough moisture in the air, the plant produces petioles (leaf stalks) that harden into sharp spines. Small oval leaves two inches (5 cm) in diameter sprout from the base of the spines. Unlike plants in wetter climates, ocotillos and some other desert specialists photosynthesize using their stems instead of their leaves. This "idling metabolism" allows them to leaf out and begin to photosynthesize quickly after rains, in contrast to many other plants that go into dormancy during dry seasons.

Sky islands

Karin Lakshmi von May, illustrator

In the Santa Catalina Mountains of southeastern Arizona, the iridescent blue gorget of the male **blue-throated mountain-gem** *(Lampornis clemenciae)* catches the light. Up to five inches (8 cm) long, the mountain gem is the largest hummingbird north of Mexico and weighs more than three times as much as the ruby-throat. Like other hummingbirds in the Trochilidae family, they're attracted to red and pink flowers, such as the tall arching green stems and coral-pink flowers of the **red yucca** *(Hesperaloe parviflora)*.

Although the female doesn't have a blue throat, both sexes have slightly curved dark bills, bronzy-green coloring around their head and shoulders, a rich gray body, and a blue-black tail with white corners. They can be easily identified in the field by white stripes above and below the eye. Blue-throated mountain-gems use vocalizations, instead of the more typical hummingbird aerial display, to defend their territory and attract mates. Both males and females have complex songs and may sing in duet during courtship. They can be aggressive when guarding their nectar sources or fighting off much larger predatory birds, like northern goshawks.

The **velvet mesquite tree** *(Prosopis velutina)* is a native species of Southern Arizona and grows in desert washes and at lower elevations. Mesquites grow up to 30 feet (9 m) tall and provide food and cover for birds, attract bees and other insects, and offer a nesting spot to migratory songbirds. Mesquite trees have roots that tap into the water table both shallowly and again at a much deeper level, giving it the ability to sustain itself in periods of both heavy and low rainfall. Mesquite forests or "bosques" once lined the Verde and other similar areas.

In the summer months, the blue-throated mountain-gem follows monsoon rains north as it migrates among the Madrean sky islands like the Catalina Mountains in Southeastern Arizona. Sky islands are one of the most biodiverse regions in the world, and are home to many endemic species found nowhere else.

A colorful invader

Sami Hernandez, illustrator

The hibiscus flower and the **gold dust day gecko *(Phelsuma laticauda)*** are a dazzle of tropical colors. Groups of these little geckos often congregate together on one plant in a "lounge of lizards." These diurnal day geckos are green with a dusting of gold speckles on their neck, shoulders, and tail. Their eyes are brown ringed with blue eyelids, they have orange or red bars across their head and similarly colored spots just to the fore of their rear legs.

The **Chinese hibiscus *(Hibiscus rosa-sinensis)*** is known for its large, open-petaled, scentless flowers that have been bred in a variety of bright colors. The center upright style contains both male (stamen) and female (pistil) reproductive organs. Bees, butterflies, and hummingbirds are their main pollinators, but the little geckos favor them too. The geckos climb into the blossoms of the hibiscus and reach the nectar with their narrow snouts and long tongues. Along the way, they pick up pollen grains on their scales, and carry them off to pollinate the next blossom.

The gold dust day gecko is not a native of Hawai'i. It was illegally smuggled in by a University of Hawai'i student in 1974 who released eight of these lizards. They dispersed and colonized on their own and now are found in gardens and wild areas in south and central Maui. The full effect of introducing the new colorful lizards to the delicate native ecosystem is not yet understood, although it clearly presents a danger to native animals, which they outcompete.

An argument of anoles

Megan Wilson, illustrator

The **green anole *(Anolis carolinensis)*** is slender, scaly, and has feet with adhesive pads allowing it to climb without slipping. This small lizard is often seen on fences and the sides of trees and buildings. Green anoles change color from brown to bright green, according to their activity level, health, mood, and dominance, rather than as a form of camouflage.

Male anoles are bigger than females and have a larger bright red or pink throat fan called a dewlap, which they use for display. Males are territorial and are willing to fight to defend their territories, even squaring off against their own reflection.

Anoles are insect eaters, but they are also known to enjoy sugary treats, raiding hummingbird feeders and drinking nectar from palms like the **saw palmetto *(Serenoa repens)*.** Saw palmetto has fan-shaped fronds and spring blooms of three foot (1 m) long flower stalks with nectar-filled yellow-white flowers that butterflies and bees love. Saw palmetto honey comes from these flowers. Their fruit starts out green, turns orange, and finally ripens to a rich black.

Anoles, like many lizards, have autotomic tails that they can cast off at will and that still wriggle when broken off. The discarded tail may distract the predator, and, while it will regenerate, it will never grow back as long or as flexible as the original one.

Once in a lifetime
Erin Packard, illustrator

Mexican long-tongued bats *(Choeronycteris mexicana)* can be found from the southwestern U.S. through Mexico and Central America. These cave dwellers are seasonal migrators. After breeding in the southwest in the summer, they migrate to Mexico and Central America in the fall. They are three to four inches (7.5-10 cm) long, have a wingspan of up to 14 inches (35.5 cm), weigh less than a ¹⁄₁₀ of an ounce (3 g), and are grayish brown. Their long tongues, for which they are named, have the capacity to extend more than a third of their body length and enable them to feed while hovering.

They forage on the nectar and pollen of night-blooming plants, favoring agave and columnar cacti, and incidentally consume insects in the process. Many species of plants depend on these important pollinators for pollination. These relationship are being threatened by climate change and habitat destruction, as well as cave tourism, putting both the bats and plants at risk.

Century plants *(Agave americana)* are succulents that require very little water to survive. The term century plant is a bit of an exaggeration. Agaves live 10 to 30 years, but they only flower once in their lives. Gathering and storing energy, they put out an impressive display, rapidly growing a giant 15 to 30 foot (4.5 to 9 m) stem from their silvery blue-green leaf rosette. On this candelabra-shaped stem, the agave produces a large number of tubular yellow flowers filled with nectar that bloom at night, attracting bats and moths. The flowers open for about a month, then the main plant dies, survived by its seeds and offshoots.

The sugary agave stalks, which weigh several pounds, can be roasted and eaten. The dried stalks have been used to make didgeridoos while the sap of the blue agave is used to produce tequila.

Hovering under the stars

Sami Hernandez, illustrator

In the early evening in the desert, as the sky turns dark and the stars come out, a small creature with dark eyes and honey-brown fur hovers over a flower of the giant cardon cactus flower. This is the **lesser long-nosed bat** *(Leptonycteris yerbabuenae),* one of only a few pollinating bats in the United States.

Its extendible three inch (7.5 cm) tongue is the same length as its body, and, as it drinks nectar, its furry head and snout get covered in golden pollen. These bats fulfill an important role as pollinators of saguaros, agaves, organ pipes, and cardon cacti, as well as other night-blooming plants. They spend winters in central Mexico and then migrate, following the nectar trail and the scent of blooming flowers, north into the southwestern United States.

The **cardon cactus** *(Pachycereus pringlei)* is the tallest cactus in the world and one of the longest-living. Some have grown to 60 feet (18.3 m) high and lived up to 200 years. They form multiple branches close to the base, giving them long, straight, vertical arms. Groups of mature cardons can form communities or forests called cardonals. In the spring, the tips of the older branches produce buds which bloom into large flowers. While each flower remains open for only 24 hours, the cactus can flower for three to four weeks as the buds mature at different times. Bees visit the flowers by day and bats by night.

A member of the leaf-nosed bat family, like the Mexican long-tongued bat, the lesser long-nosed bat has a triangular flap of skin shaped like a leaf at the end of its nose. Their leaf-like nose shape may have evolved to aid their echolocation.

Scrappy pioneers
Madi Henline, illustrator

The **common opossum** *(Didelphis marsupialis)* is found from the northern part of South America to the southern part of Mexico, where it meets the lower range of its cousin, the Virginia opossum. About the size of a house cat, it has a cream-colored face with dark eye stripes and forehead, a pink nose, and black ears. Its shaggy coat contains different tones of grays, blacks, and yellows. Opossums are excellent climbers, aided by a long, prehensile tail and an opposable hallux, or thumb, on all four paws.

Like their northern cousins, the common opossum is an opportunistic generalist—an omnivore that takes advantage of a range of foods and habitats. During its nocturnal incursions, it hunts small prey, scavenges carrion, and munches on leaves, fruit, and nectar from plants.

The **canudeiro** *(Mabea fistulifera)* blooms during Brazil's dry season, when food resources are scarce. For the three nights of each inflorescence's bloom, it provides large amounts of pollen and nectar to passing pollinators. Canudeiro plants are monoecious, which means they have male and female flowers in separate structures on the same plant. In a typical inflorescence or cluster of flowers, there are about three to twelve pistillate female flowers and 350 or so male staminate flowers. Their small berry-like flowers are at first a dull yellow green, then turn bright pinkish red.

The canudeiro is a hardy pioneer species that can thrive in landscapes damaged or disturbed by fire, storms, or construction. Pioneer species can withstand harsh conditions. They reach reproductive maturity quickly and their presence increases diversity in a region. The pollinators of these species become similarly vital to the survival of an ecosystem.

Contributors

ERIN AVERY, *Sweeping up pollen, p. 55*
gnsi-carolinas.com/erin-avery | @eringavery.art on Instagram

Erin Avery is an artist and illustrator based in Raleigh, NC, working primarily in ink and watercolor. Her art is rooted in a lifelong fascination with nature, and she is particularly interested in insects, native plants, and their conservation. She has a degree in Archeology from Western Kentucky University and has volunteered with the North Carolina Science Museum. She is currently serving as secretary for the Carolinas chapter of the Guild of Natural Science Illustrators.

CASS GRAYBEAL BROWN, *The body language of bees, p. 57*
grayillu.com

Cassandra Brown majored in Illustration at Savannah College of Art and Design. While in school, she focused on and minored in scientific illustration. Currently she is located in upstate NY with her husband and pit bull. The rich landscape and vibrant wildlife that surrounds them fuels the creativity behind her traditional scientific style.

ALISON BURKE, *Unlocking hidden treasure, p. 61*
alison-burke.com | aminocreative.com

Alison Burke is an award-winning Senior Medical/Scientific Illustrator at the *New England Journal of Medicine* (NEJM) in Boston, MA, and a partner for Amino Creative, LLC. Prior to joining NEJM, she was a Senior Medical Illustrator at the *Journal of the American Medical Association*. Alison holds a M.A. in Medical and Biological Illustration degree from Johns Hopkins University School of Medicine, and a B.S. in Animal Science and Entomology degree from Cornell University. A professional member and Fellow of the Association of Medical Illustrators (AMI), she received the AMI's Outstanding Achievement Award in 2014. She's also a member of the Guild of Natural Science Illustrators. She enjoys illustrating a wide variety of subjects and has a special interest in insects and life cycles.

C OLIVIA CARLISLE, *Changing with the seasons, p. 27*
carlisleillustration.squarespace.com
@oc4artist on Twitter | @occarlisle on Instagram

Enchanted by her mother's and grandmother's gardens in Athens, GA, and with a talent for drawing and painting, the seeds were planted for C Olivia to flourish in scientific illustration. She cultivated her creative skills through classes, photography, illustration, and graphic design in federal government careers. Olivia designed her American University Interdisciplinary B.A. degree program in visual communications, the first of its kind, and studied Scientific Illustration at the University of Georgia. She shares her skills through workshops for children and adults. In 2018, Olivia co-founded the GNSI Georgia Group. She serves on the *Journal of Natural Science Illustration* and has had work featured in GNSI juried exhibitions.

Contributors

CARRIE CARLSON, *Darwin was right, p. 45; Up in the clouds, p 63*
cscarlson.com | @bluebirdprintstudios

Carrie Carlson earned a BA in Biology and Art from Luther College, an MFA in Scientific Illustration from the University of Michigan, and an MA in Printmaking from Governors State University. Since 2001, she has been a full-time high school educator near Chicago. She has split her years between the science and art departments; teaching Drawing, Painting, International Baccalaureate Visual Arts, as well as Biology, Biomedical Sciences, and Horticulture. She also teaches a variety of adult art courses at the Morton Arboretum, including linoleum block printing, drawing birds, and field sketching.

SARA LYNN CRAMB, *Feeding every few minutes, p. 97*
saralynncramb.com | @saralynncreative on Instagram

Sara is a freelance illustrator and designer living in Fairbanks, AK. She creates work for educational children's publications, websites, mobile apps, and museums with a focus on engaging and educating young audiences about the natural world. Curious about animals and nature since childhood, she sneaks off for outdoor adventures whenever possible. Travel and nature offer an abundance of inspiration for her work and she is always excited to learn more about the fascinating world around us. She enjoys sketching with traditional media and finishes her work in Adobe Illustrator and Procreate. Sara has worked on numerous children's books including *If You Are a Kaka, You Eat Doo Doo; Search the Ocean: Find the Animals;* and *Smithsonian Young Explorers Fact Book & Floor Puzzle: 50 States.*

CAROL CREECH, *Generating heat, wind, and odor, p. 17*
ccreechstudio.com

Carol Creech is a nature illustrator and maker based in Ann Arbor, MI. She enjoys creating with a variety of materials and her work includes traditional botanical and nature illustrations, natural stone jewelry and handmade journals. She holds a BA in Geography, an MILS in Library and Information Studies, and has taken courses at the Brookside Gardens School of Botanical Art and Illustration. She is a member of the Guild of Natural Science Illustrators (GNSI) and the American Society of Botanical Artists and has exhibited locally at Matthaei Botanical Gardens and regionally with other GNSI Great Lakes artists.

JENNIFER DEUTSCHER, *Lured and trapped, p. 13*
alithographica.com

Jennifer (Jenn) Deutscher is a scientific illustrator from Phoenix, AZ, currently based in NYC. Part scientist and part artist, Jenn is fundamentally curious about how things work and uses her art to document her observations and encourage viewers to rethink the world around them. She holds a B.A. in biological sciences and illustration from New York University, where she also worked for several years as a genetics research assistant. She also received a certificate in botanical art and illustration from the New York Botanical Garden. Her work has appeared in galleries, museum exhibits, scientific journals, and educational materials internationally.

Contributors

AISSA DOMINGO, *A link to the divine, p. 59; The vegetarian wasp, p. 73*
aissadomingo.com | @aissa_domingo on Instagram

Aissa Domingo is an artist, photographer, and illustrator from the Zoology Division at the National Museum of the Philippines. Since 2010, her scientific illustrations and photographs of animals, plants, and fossils have been published in several local and international scientific journals. She led the reconstructive painting of both the replica and actual taxidermy specimen of "Lolong," a famous giant crocodile along with taxidermists, researchers, and scientists. As an artist in a scientific institution, she developed her skill in understanding the synergy between the sciences and the arts and the convergence of these important disciplines, for a better appreciation of the wealth and beauty of the natural history of the Philippines. She studied Painting and graduated cum laude from the University of Santo Tomas, Manila.

VICKY EARLE, *Tiger-striped enchantment, p. 23*
Drawinnature.com | @DrawInNature on Instagram and twitter

Vicky Earle is a freelance natural science / medical illustrator and artist for conservation from Vancouver, Canada. Her love affair with nature started at just 6 months of age when she made a mad dash for Lake Superior. Her parents caught her as tiny fingers touched the water. That exhilaration has stayed with Vicky a lifetime. She is very passionate about the planet and connecting people to nature through art. Working primarily in watercolor, her work focuses on sharing the stories and intelligence of our natural world. Vicky graduated from the University of Toronto with a degree in Medical Illustration/Biocommunications, received a Master's in Education Technology from the University of British Columbia, and holds a certificate in natural history illustration from the University of Newcastle.

SUSAN FOX, *A delight of color, p. 53; Chasing the blooms, p. 93*
foxstudio.biz | sketchwild.com
Facebook, Instagram, Twitter, Pinterest, Etsy and RedBubble

Susan Fox has worked in art-related fields for over forty years. For the last twenty, she's mostly painted in oil, specializing in animals and the natural world. A world traveler, she keeps sketchbooks of her travels, including trips to Mongolia, Kenya, Europe, and locations in the US. She has a BFA in Illustration from the Academy of Art University in San Francisco. She lives on an acre in redwood country in northern CA with her husband, two rough collie dogs, and two cats.

SAMANTHA GALLAGHER, *Color-coded rewards, p. 41*
The bees in the willows, p. 51
samanthagallagherillustration.com | @sammybeezz on Instagram

Samantha Gallagher is a freelance scientific and nature illustrator in Illinois. She has a BA in Graphic Design from Flagler College and a MS degree in Entomology from the University of Florida. She has been a bee enthusiast since she was very young, filling her bedroom walls with her drawings of bees. Now, as an adult, she continues to do the same thing to the walls of her studio. On a larger scale, she paints murals. When she is not drawing or painting insects, she is working on bee identification and taxonomy with her microscope. Her preferred mediums are colored pencils, ink, and acrylic painting. Her goal is to encourage people to notice the beauty of insects that they may have otherwise disliked or dismissed, hoping to invoke feelings of curiosity and compassion.

Contributors

MADISON HENLINE, *Scrappy pioneers, p. 115*
madisonhenline.com, @rhunevild on Instagram and Twitter

Though currently based in Dallas, TX, Madison grew up in Savannah, Georgia and attended SCAD. She graduated with a degree in Sequential Art, though these days she focuses more on paleoart and sculpture than comic books.

CHARON HENNING, *Costas hummingbirds on agave (copyright page); Tiny muse, p. 99; Desert blooms p. 103*
charonhenning.com, keiphavian.com

Charon Henning is a location-independent scientific illustrator and fine artist. A member of the Guild of Natural Science Illustrators, she enjoys working in the areas of vertebrate paleontology, osteology and ornithology in a variety of media. She holds an Associate's Degree in Fine Art from Prince George's Community College and a Bachelor's Degree in Individualized Studies: Multimedia Storytelling from George Mason University, where she earned the faculty award for Most Creative Capstone Project.

SAMI HERNANDEZ, *Planting for the future, p. 67*
A colorful invader, p. 107 and featured on the back cover
Hovering under the stars, p. 113
samihernandez.com | @petite_sami on Instagram & Artstation

Samantha 'Sami' Hernandez is an eco-conscious cat mom of three and digital artist residing in North Texas. This is the third coloring book her artwork has been featured in and she is very proud of the goals, artistic expression, and educational value of these books. While her degree helped her to create her children's book, *Fleet Saves the Prince*, Sami also enjoys working on character designs and illustrations that help her expand her skillsets as she enters the fantasy genre.

CHELSEA HOUSAND, *A world in miniture, p. 9*
The misleading moth, p. 43
housandarts.com | @housandarts

Chelsea is a full time illustrator and designer from a small town on the Eastern Shore of Maryland. She primarily works in the music industry making posters and merchandise for live entertainment as well as curating a small online shop. She loves to combine her passion for nature with her professional practice at any chance possible. Chelsea recently received her BFA in Illustration with a concentration in Surface Design from Savannah College of Art and Design.

Contributors

CLARA HUNT, *A sure sign of spring, p. 91*
@clara_fied27 on Instagram

Clara Hunt is an illustrator based in Atlanta, Georgia. After moving from Southeast Wisconsin to pursue an art education at Savannah College of Art and Design, she found her passion in creating work for children. Clara is constantly inspired by bluegrass music, her eclectic friends, and educational nature projects like this!

MARIA KLOS, *A one-day bloom, p. 37*
@makillustration on Instagram

Maria Klos is an aspiring scientific illustrator who creates illustrations of observations from the natural world, largely focusing on animals and plants. Recently receiving her BA degree from Arcadia University, Maria will be attending California State University Monterey Bay for a post-graduate program in scientific illustration. As an illustrator, Maria's goal is to educate and inspire wonder for the natural world through her artwork.

KARIN LAKSHMI VON MAY, *On gossamer wings, p. 33*
Intensely active just above ground, p. 69; A courtship duet, p. 105
karinvonmay.com | @karin.von.may on instagram

Karin von May is a Tucson, AZ based artist and natural science illustrator. Her illustrations, distinct in their celebration of detailed observations and thoughtful artistry, are intricate visual tributes to the transcendent beauty of her current subjects: the rich flora and fauna endemic to upland Sonoran Desert. Von May's worldview and art practice reflect the profound influence of her multicultural upbringing in the Bay Area and Peru's Brow of the Amazon.

MATTIAS LANAS, *False advertising, p. 65*
mattiaslanas.com | @mattiasillustration on Instagram

Mattias Lanas is a Chilean-American artist based in Bogotá, Colombia. He is passionate about the intersection of art, natural sciences, and education and loves spending his weekends outdoors "botanizing" or doing ceramics. He holds a BS and MS in Earth Systems from Stanford University (2012) and completed California State University, Monterey Bay's graduate program in Scientific Illustration in 2015. In 2019-2020 he was a Fulbright Scholar at the Muséum National d'Histoire Naturelle in Paris. Lanas is a freelance illustrator, has taught natural science illustration classes at the high school and college level, and is now adventuring around the world with his spouse in the diplomatic service.

Contributors

TAINA LITWAK, *Anatomy of a flower, p. 1; Swimming in snow melt, p. 11; Who likes flattops?, p. 21; A healthy co-dependence, p. 35*
litwakillustration.com | @LitwakIllustration on Facebook
science-art.com/member/?id=31#.YIbkxuspDm0

Taina Litwak, CMI, is a scientific and board certified medical illustrator. Originally from NY, she attended the University of CT for a BS in Biology and a BFA. She has been a full-time illustrator for 39 years, primarily in the Washington DC area. Traditionally trained, she made the transition to illustrating digitally in the 90s. She's fond of marine invertebrates and has dedicated most of her career to taxonomic entomological illustration for federally funded scientists at the Museum of Natural History at the Smithsonian Institution. She's volunteered extensively and served on the Boards of Directors of the Guild of Natural Science Illustrators, the Vesalius Trust, the Illustrator's Club of Washington, and the American Society of Collective Rights Licensing.

HANNAH LOEFFELHOLZ, *Bumblebee, table of contents and page numbers; Night and day over the waves, p. 101*
spoonwoodvisuals.com | @spoonwoodvisuals on Instagram and Facebook

Hannah Loeffelholz is a scientific illustrator and creator of fine art based in Rochester, MN, where she lives with her boyfriend and their two pets, a cat and dog. Most of Hannah's work focuses on raising awareness for endangered species, as well as capturing the unique forms of birds and reptiles. Hannah spends her weekends traveling and hiking in search of viewpoints from which to sketch and photograph Minnesota's beautiful natural scenery. She graduated in May 2020 from Iowa State University with a Bachelor's Degree in Biological/Pre-Medical Illustration.

BEA MARTIN, *From the earliest days, p. 83; The ultimate survivors, p. 87*
bmartinvisualswordpress.com

Bea Martin is a character animator as well as a certified medical illustrator (CMI), urban sketcher, nature journal enthusiast and educator based in Vancouver, BC. After earning a medical degree from the Universidad Complutense de Madrid in Spain, a Fulbright Scholarship allowed her to pursue a MA in Biological and Medical Illustration at The Johns Hopkins University School of Medicine. She later relocated to Canada to study animation. With curiosity and enthusiasm, Bea loves crafting entertaining, inspiring, and educational stories, merging art with science. She loves sketching outdoors and finding interesting opportunities to continue learning. She also supports creativity and artistic development in children through nature journal workshops.

CLAIRE ALDERKS MILLER, *The eater of insects, p. 81*
clairealderksmiller.com

Claire Miller is a botanical/nature artist and illustrator living in Raleigh, NC. She is inspired by the natural world and the diverse plant world of NC in particular. Nature's shapes, with their color, light and shadows intrigue her. Sketching from life, she also researches and photographs her subjects from different angles. She wants accuracy, but likes to play with the compostion and color to highlight their form and beauty. Claire has degrees in Biology and Studio Art from the Univ. of Richmond, a Botanical Illustration Certificate from the NC Botanical Garden, and professional experience as a graphic and freelance artist. She mainly works in watercolor, colored pencil on film, or mixed media with watercolor and colored pencil.

Contributors

TIFFANY MILLER RUSSELL, AUTHOR
Wandering lover, p. 7; An ancient pact, p. 85
wildlifeinpaper.com

Tiffany Miller Russell has a love for the unique and unusual that has led her to study the natural world and depict it in cut paper sculpture. Her paper sculptures have won her numerous awards from the likes of Artists' Magazine and the Society of Animal Artists, including a travel grant to Trinidad and Tobago. She shows regularly in juried museum exhibitions and fine art galleries, and two of her works are included in the permanent Contemporary Art collection of the Cheyenne Frontier Days Old West Museum. She resides in Denver, CO.

CHRISTINA SPENCE MORGAN, *Under the microscope, p. 3*
christinamorganillustration.com

Christina Spence Morgan is an early-career illustrator originally from the Florida panhandle, and currently based in the DC area. She earned her BS in Marine Biology from the University of California Santa Cruz in 2007, and a Professional Certificate in Museum Studies from CU Boulder in 2010. She has worked in both natural history museum collections and in aquarium animal husbandry, with her illustration expertise including marine biology, paleobiology, and botany. She is also a proud Navy wife, and mother to two little busy bees of her own. She loves drawing the details of nature, and showing the worlds within worlds.

CORDELIA NORRIS, AUTHOR, *Under the sea, p. 5*
lunacreates.com | @localloveboutique on Etsy

Cordelia is lead creative and founder of Luna Creative, an award-winning design and illustration studio dedicated to creating a cleaner, more sustainable future, now celebrating its 11th year. She has a Master's in Illustration from SCAD and undergraduate degrees in Graphic Design, Studio Art, and Art History. Her work's been recognized with awards from American Institute of Graphic Artists (AIGA), American Advertising Federation (AAF), *Applied Arts*, and exhibited around the country. She lives in Wilmington, NC, with her adorable family (husband, little boy, dog, and cat). She lauched the Coloring Wonder series in 2018 with the release of *Hatchlings*, followed by *All Along the Atlantic* in 2019. This is her third coloring book in the Coloring Wonder series.

LAURIE O'KEEFE, *Island marble butterfly and mustard plant (dedication page)*
laurieokeefe.com

Laurie O'Keefe has been working as an independent contractor specializing in medical, and biological topics for over 30 years. She earned a B.S. in zoology, and an M.S. in anatomy, with a concentration in biomedical illustration from Colorado State University. Her illustration career has included a large range of subjects and clients, including textbook illustration for all educational levels, medical product art, natural science exhibits at the Smithsonian and Oklahoma Museum of Natural History, editorial work for journals, magazines, and scientific websites, children's books, greeting cards, and medical legal malpractice and personal injury trial art. She currently lives and works from her home studio on Orcas Island, WA. Her favorite subjects revolve around animals and natural topics, but she is most known for her veterinary illustration and depiction of creatures "inside and out".

Contributors

ERIN PACKARD, *Hovering under the stars, p. 111*
@epackart on Instagram

Erin Packard is a freelance artist from Boston, MA. She studied illustration at SCAD and at MassArt, and spends much of her free time admiring and sketching Boston's urban wildlife. Her artistic interests range from natural science to children's book illustration and beyond. The majority of her work explores the natural world and human impact upon it, but her favorite subjects might still be her own pets.

DORIE PETROCHKO, *Ruby-throated hummingbird and Sakura cherry blossoms (title page spread)*
doriepetrochko-studio.com, ctnsi.com

Traveling and painting birds to benefit bird conservation is a lifelong passion for Dorie. She is committed to using her talents to educate people about our changing environment and the need to protect its species worldwide. Dorie is an award-winning wildlife painter who has exhibited and published her work nationally and internationally. She is the recipient of the Don Eckelberry Fellowship for wildlife painting, the Julia and David White Artist Fellowship in Costa Rica, and the Big Cypress National Park artist residency in Florida. She holds a Masters in Art Education from Southern Connecticut State University and a certificate in Botanical and Natural Science Illustration from the New York Botanical Garden. A founding instructor of the Peabody Museum of Natural History's Natural Science Illustration Program, Dorie teaches classes in drawing, watercolor, mixed media, and colored pencil and is an active member and exhibitor of the Guild of Natural Science Illustrators.

TRUDY SMOKE ROBBINS, AUTHOR, *The well-bred moth, p. 39*
http://drawingonthenaturalworld.blogspot.com/

Trudy Smoke Robbins is a nature illustrator and earned a certificate in Botanical Illustration from the New York Botanical Garden in 2019. She illustrated Field Guide to the Neighborhood Birds of New York City (2015) and Field Guide to the Street Trees of New York City (2011) both by Leslie Day and published by Johns Hopkins University Press. She is Professor Emerita from Hunter College, CUNY, Department of English where she taught linguistics and rhetoric. She loves learning about nature and working collaboratively, so working on this book has given her enormous joy.

LAUREN ROSENFELT, *Perennially popular, p. 77; Dinner and a date, p. 79*
laurenrosenfelt.com

Lauren is a natural science illustrator and conceptual artist currently living and working in Norman, OK. She graduated from USAO in 2014 with a BFA and minor in Liberal Arts. She learned the essentials of managing an artistic business while working with Shevaun Williams. In 2020, she started to work for herself and focus on her artistic practice full time. Her work focuses on the importance of native wildlife species and she contributes to her community and state through promoting habitat restoration efforts. Currently, she's working on an educational and artistic signage project for the Norman Central Library to raise awareness to the importance of the library's miniature mixed grass prairie and water retention landscape.

Contributors

CARLA SCHMAKEL, *Clouded and orange sulphurs, red clover, and helianthus (half title page); Nectar thieves, p. 25; Grasshopper hunter, p. 75*
natureartistsguild.com/featured-artist/carla-schmakel-spring-2014/

Carla Schmakel is a nature artist inspired by the rare plant and animal communities of the Chicago Region, surrounding southern Lake Michigan. She began to draw while planting a home habitat garden with her spouse in Lake County, IL. Their garden is certified in the Illinois Audubon Society's Bird and Butterfly Sanctuary program. She participates in citizen science monitoring programs, include the Illinois Butterfly Monitoring Network, Bird Conservation Network, Sharing Our Shore-Lake County Audubon Society, Plants of Concern, and is a restoration volunteer with the Lake County Forest Preserve District.

CAROL SCHWARTZ, *Fuzzy flies, p. 15; The all-in-one cactus, p. 95*
csillustration.com

Carol Schwartz lives in Connecticut and had taught at a number of universities and colleges. Most recently she is an Assistant Professor in Illustration at The University of Hartford. She studied at the Kansas City Art Institute, Rhode Island School of Design and has a MFA from the University of Hartford. Her award-winning science and nature illustrations from 60 picture books spark wonder for children. Her paintings have been included in exhibitions throughout the country. She combines gouache and digital illustration to create her work and finds joy in bringing attention to the small things in nature and painting them in great detail. Sea life, insects, and botanicals are Carol's favorite subjects to illustrate.

DEB SHAW, *Siren scent, p. 19*
dbshawstudios.com

Deborah Shaw has a degree in fine art from Pomona College, The Claremont Colleges, where she studied botany and native California flora. She is the principal of dbShaw Studios, an award-winning, multi-disciplinary design company, specializing in print, information design, web design, illustration, and scientific illustration. Ms. Shaw is an active member of the the Guild of Natural Science Illustrators, the American Society of Botanical Artists (ASBA), the Botanical Artists Guild of Southern California, the Northern California Society of Botanical Artists, and the Southwest Society of Botanical Artists. Her work has been exhibited internationally, and is in permanent museum collections, and private collections. She teaches internationally, and has received numerous awards for art, illustration, and design. She's the recipient of the 2020 ASBA James White Service Award for Dedication to Botanical Art and a contributor to the ASBA publication, *Botanical Art Techniques* by ASBA, Carol Woodin, and Robin Jess.

GABRIELA SINCICH, *The beetle that purrs, p. 89*
gabrielasincich.com

Gabriela is a visual artist living in Indiana. Her work is primarily influenced by the natural world and she is especially inspired by plants, insects, and birds. She studied Fine Arts and Visual Arts Education at the University of Córdoba, Argentina. Soon after her graduation she started doing illustrations for science in collaboration with her husband, biologist Esteban Fernandez-Juricic, which provided her the opportunity to work on a variety of natural science illustration projects, from illustrations for publications and collaborations with environmental agencies to the development of outreach programs to promote understanding and respect for the natural world through art.

Contributors

AMANDA SURVESKI, *Golden skies, p. 31*
The bountiful thistle, p. 49, and featured on the cover
amandasurveski.com

Amanda Surveski is a freelance artist based in central Connecticut. In 2017, she received a degree in illustration from Savannah College of Art and Design. Since then, she has been working as an established freelance artist, creating graphic and illustrative content for a number of clients. She focuses her work on native New England wildlife, highlighting the abundance of nature within the area. Her work is continually featured in galleries across the U.S. and worldwide. When not working in the studio, you can find her outside, taking way too many photos of plants and animals.

AMELIA SVEC, *Good medicine, p. 29*
Ameliacatherineillustration.com
@ameliacatherineillustration on Facebook

Amelia Svec is a freelance illustrator in the Grand Traverse region of Northern Michigan. Amelia loves illustrating nature, specifically focusing on the overlooked and unnoticed; keeping her illustrations both scientifically accurate for educational purposes, as well as aesthetically beautiful to emphasise the beautiful design of all life and to encourage wonder as well as appreciation. Insects in particular are her favorite subject matter to draw because of their incredible diversity and unique ecological purposes. Bugs, birds, and botanicals are all on display throughout Amelia's illustrations. Amelia received her BFA degree from Grand Valley State University, with an emphasis in illustration and biology.

COURTNEY WERNER, *Invader in the nest, p. 71*
@courtneywerner on Instagram

Courtney is a postbaccalaureate researcher and artist based in Durham, NC. She feels deeply connected to Southern Appalachian and Piedmont ecosystems, and she explores the unique forms that live there through her scientific and artistic practice. She completed coursework in ecology, evolution, and illustration at Duke University and remains devoted to independent naturalist study. Courtney is pursuing a research career in ecology and conservation and will continue using art and design to communicate scientific concepts with diverse audiences.

MEGAN WILSON, *Attack of the caterpillars, p. 47*
An argument of anolis, p. 109
meywilson.wixsite.com/eusocialmedia | @eusocialmeg on Twitter

Growing up in a small town along the Appalachian trail, Megan developed a passion for collecting biological specimens and studying the natural world. She's currently completing a doctoral degree in Biology based out of Rutgers-Newark University and the American Museum of Natural History, and her work focuses on evolutionary biology and phylogenetics of insects. She's particularly interested in the social evolution of termites, and the unique forms and patterns observed across insect societies. She has traveled to the rainforests of South America and Australia for her work, collecting insects and observing the pristine natural beauty of these regions. She will be starting a new journey as a Naval Officer of Entomology, serving her country and connecting entomological research directly with global health and our nation's troops.

CPSIA information can be obtained
at www.ICGtesting.com
Printed in the USA
LVHW070007201221
706671LV00003B/5